Michael & Bernice .

NO RINGY, NO DINGY

**Save Yourself A Whole Lot Of Heartache;
It Is Time To Fulfil Destiny.
Prevention Is Better Than Cure!!!**

HWP

NO RINGY, NO DINGY
ISBN 978-0-9562541-8-4

In the UK write to:
Michael Hutton-Wood Ministries
P. O. Box 1226, Croydon. CR9 6DG.

Or in the UK
Call: Tel. 020 8689 6010; 07956 815 714
Outside the UK call: +44 20 8689 6010; +44 7956 815 714

Or contact:
Website: www.houseofjudah.org.uk
Email: michaelhutton-wood@fsmail.net
        houseofjudah@ymail.com
        leadersfactoryinternational@yahoo.com

Published & distributed by: Michael Hutton-Wood Ministries
(Incorporating Hutton-Wood World Outreach Ministries)

THE MANDATE:

'...SET IN ORDER THE THINGS THAT ARE OUT OF ORDER AND RAISE AND APPOINT LEADERS IN EVERY CITY.' - Titus 1:5

MICHAEL HUTTON-WOOD MINISTRIES

RELEASING POTENTIAL
- MAXIMIZING DESTINY

HOUSE OF JUDAH (PRAISE) MINISTRIES
&
LEADERS FACTORY INTERNATIONAL

RAISING GENERATIONAL LEADERS
- IMPACTING NATIONS

SIMPA:

SCEPTRE INTERNATIONAL MINISTERS & PASTORS ASSOCIATION

EQUIPPING, EMPOWERING, COACHING, MENTORING AND PROVIDING COVERING FOR PASTORS, MINISTERS AND LEADERS ACROSS THE NATIONS!

CONTENTS

INTRODUCTION

It is better to build a fence on top of a cliff than a hospital the bottom of a cliff. Prevention is better than cure.

NO RINGY, NO DINGY simply means: Don't light certain fires before their time or that same fire will burn you. It is better to try to keep a bad thing from happening than it is to fix the bad thing once it has happened. An ounce of prevention is better than a pound of cure.

This book has been written to help singles or those who have suffered from previous broken relationships out of ignorance, being forced into relationships or those stepping out afresh into relationships not to make the mistakes of previous generations but LOOK BEFORE THEY LEAP!

In this book, you will discover the following:
-   How to forget the past and press on!

-   30 Facts about your Past vs. Your Future

-   How your choices affect and determine your future

-   60 Keys to Designing Your Future

-   WHY AND WHAT IS ABSTINENCE?

-   40 Benefits of Abstinence

-   21 Important Facts about Abstinence

- HOW TO AVOID, RESIST AND OVERCOME TEMPTATION

- 21 Facts about Temptation

- 30 things To Know about Temptation

- 30 Do's and Don'ts

- WHAT IS MARRIAGE?

- 101 REASONS WHY PEOPLE MARRY

- WHAT EVERY ONE SHOULD KNOW ABOUT DIVORCE BEFORE THEY GET MARRIED

- HOW TO MAKE THE RIGHT CHOICE OF A MARRIAGE PARTNER

- 21 Characteristics of a Disciplined Life

- How God Brings Your Partner [21 Factors to Consider]

- 21 Facts About Right and Wrong Thinking/Thoughts

- 120 Mandatory Questions to Ask and Investigate

- ADVICE TO PROSPECTIVE COUPLES & THOSE IN COURTSHIP

- THE CHECKLIST: 100 key Characteristics to look for in a potential spouse

IT IS TIME TO FULFILL DESTINY BY MAKING RIGHT CHOICES CULMINATING IN GOOD DECISIONS. NO RINGY, NO DINGY!!!!!
Shalom!

REMEMBER THIS:

'We all have two choices.
We can make a living or we can design a life.'
– Jim Rohn

UNTIL THE PRESCRIBED
PRE-REQUISITES ARE MET FULLY,
THE 'GATE' MUST REMAIN CLOSED
PERMANENTLY!

Nobody is under obligation not to tempt you - you are under obligation not to yield to temptation or place yourself in environments where you can be tempted to yield to it.

He who chooses the beginning of a road also chooses its outcome. So, watch what road you choose!

Right choices lead to good decisions and wrong choices lead to bad decisions.
Choose Well!

The main purpose of God for your life is
not getting married first.
IT IS TO FULFIL DESTINY!

YOUR MARRIAGE PARTNER IS
SUPPOSED TO HELP YOU FULFIL
THAT DESTINY, NOT THE OTHER
WAY ROUND!

The whole duty of man is to fear God
and obey His commands and
fulfill his vision.
(Ecclesiastes 12:13; 1 John 3:8; Jeremiah
29:11; Proverbs 29:18; 22:29; 27:8)

SECTION ONE:

WHAT TO PRIORITISE
AND PUT IN PLACE TO FULFILL
DESTINY

Chapter

One

MAKE A CONSCIOUS DECISION FOR DESTINY-FULFILMENT

The first thing to consider in the choice of a marriage partner is DESTINY. That is all that matters and that is what should ultimately dictate any move you make, career, vocation, ministry, profession you pursue and the overall choices and decisions you make in life. DESTINY!

In this book, DESTINY is actually the motivation and ethos behind and for each chapter.

WHY DESTINY?

Jeremiah 29:11, 'For I know the thoughts that I think toward you, saith the LORD, thoughts of peace, and not of evil, to give you an expected end.'

Proverbs 19:21, 'There are many devices in a man's heart; nevertheless the counsel of the LORD, that shall stand.'

Proverbs 14:12, 'There is a way which seemeth right unto a man, but the end thereof are the ways of death.'

Proverbs 27:8, 'As a bird that wandereth from her nest, so is a man that wandereth from his place.'

Psalm 32:8, 'I will instruct thee and teach thee in the way which thou shalt go: I will guide thee with mine eye.'

Isaiah 48:17, 'Thus saith the LORD, thy Redeemer, the Holy One of Israel; I am the LORD thy God which teacheth thee to profit, which leadeth thee by the way that thou shouldest go.'

The Power and Purpose of DESTINY:

1. Rob a man of his sense of destiny and you destroy his desire for living.
2. Absence of destiny is the source of depression.
3. Destiny is the source of personal and national discipline.
As we talk about destiny, it is important to define destiny:

1. Destiny is defined as the ultimate end of a thing.
2. Destiny is established purpose.
3. Destiny is the final address.
4. Destiny is the finished line of the race – the finished line

of your race.

5. Destiny is the desired result.

6. Destiny is the predetermined end of a thing

7. The reason for existence – the reason why a thing exists.

Therefore destiny is the purpose for the creation of a thing. Dr. Myles Munroe said: "I am convinced that every nation was created by God to fulfill a purpose and a destiny therefore every African, Asia, European, American, Australian nation and city was created by God to fulfill a role in the world. Oppression is designed to destroy the destiny of a people and a nation. I am also of the persuasion that your value as a nation is found in the revelation of your national destiny. Every nation was created by God to fulfill a particular destiny in the universal destiny of the world. Therefore national leaders, educators, pastors, business leaders, all national leaders must discover the nation's destiny and purpose in order to lead that nation effectively because God makes nothing without a purpose as confirmed by the apostle Paul in Acts 17:26-27, 'And hath made of one blood all nations of men for to dwell on all the face of the earth, and hath determined the times before appointed, and the bounds of their habitation; That they should seek the Lord, if haply they might feel after him, and find him, though he be not far from every one of us:'"

PLAN AND TAKE HOLD OF YOUR FUTURE

1. In life you are either planning to succeed or planning to fail!

2. HOW? – HE WHO FAILS TO PLAN IS PLANNING TO FAIL!

3. FAILURE TO PLAN = PLANNING TO FAIL!

4. LIFE DOES NOT GIVE YOU WHAT YOU DESERVE; LIFE ONLY GIVES YOU WHAT YOU DEMAND! (Matthew 11:12; Deuteronomy 2:24)

Learn from King Solomon and the ants. I came across these scriptures in my bible study this morning and I was so touched. Follow this:

Proverbs 6:6-11, **'Go to the ant, thou sluggard; consider her ways, and be wise: Which having no guide, overseer, or ruler, [or supervisor] Provideth her meat in the summer, and gathereth her food in the harvest.** How long wilt thou sleep, O sluggard? when wilt thou arise out of thy sleep? Yet a little sleep, a little slumber, a little folding of the hands to sleep: So shall thy poverty come as one that travelleth, and thy want as an armed man.'

Proverbs 30:24-28, **'There be four things which are little** upon the earth, but they are exceeding wise: The ants are a people not strong, yet they prepare their meat in the summer; The conies are but a feeble folk, yet make they their houses in the rocks; The locusts have no king, yet go they forth all of them by bands; The spider taketh hold with her hands, and is in kings' palaces.'

LESSON: NO MATTER HOW SMALL YOU ARE IN SIZE OR STATURE, NO MATTER HOW INSIGNIFICANT YOU MAY FEEL IN YOUR OWN EYES, YOU ARE ABSOLUTELY RESPONSIBLE FOR THE OUTCOME OF YOUR DESTINY BY THE CHOICES AND DECISIONS YOU MAKE IN LIFE.

Ecclesiastes 9:11, 'I returned, and saw under the sun, that the race is not to the swift, nor the battle to the strong, neither yet bread to the wise, nor yet riches to men of understanding, nor yet favour to men of skill; but time and chance happeneth to them all.'

5. DILIGENTLY PURSUE YOUR DESTINY, PURPOSE, ASSIGNMENT AND FUTURE IN LIFE: BECAUSE LIFE IS WHAT YOU MAKE IT:

Proverbs 10:4, 'He becometh poor that dealeth with a slack hand: but the hand of the diligent maketh rich.'

Proverbs 12:24, 'The hand of the diligent shall bear rule: but the slothful shall be under tribute.'

Proverbs 12:27, 'The slothful man roasteth not that which he took in hunting: but the substance of a diligent man is precious.'

Proverbs 13:4, 'The soul of the sluggard desireth, and hath nothing: but the soul of the diligent shall be made fat.'

Proverbs 21:5, 'The thoughts of the diligent tend only to plenteousness; but of every one that is hasty only to want.'

Proverbs 22:28-29, 'Remove not the ancient landmark, which thy fathers have set. Seest thou a man diligent in his business? he shall stand before kings; he shall not stand before mean men.'

6. INTELLECTUAL CAPITAL BACKED BY DIVINE WISDOM AND THE BLESSING ADDS TO YOUR OVERALL CAPITAL AND WORTH!

7. HE WHO DOES NOT PLAN HIS FUTURE IS PLANNING TO FAIL IN THE FUTURE!

8. HE WHO DOES NOT PLAN HIS FUTURE HAS NO FUTURE!

9. HE WHO DOES NOT PLAN AND PURSUE HIS FUTURE IS ALREADY DOOMED!

10. IF YOU ARE NOT PLANNING YOUR FUTURE, YOU ARE PLANNING YOUR BURIAL!

11. FAILING TO PLAN IS PLANNING TO FAIL - PERIOD!

12. IN LIFE, YOU ARE EITHER BUILDING A LIBRARY OR A MORTUARY WITHOUT KNOWING! START NOW!!!!

13. HE WHO DOES NOT GROW HIS GRASS TODAY WILL NOT EVEN HAVE GRASS TO CHEW TOMORROW!

14. YOU ARE EITHER LEAVING A LASTING MEMORY OF YOU OR WRITING YOUR OBITUARY!

15. THERE IS NO NEW THING UNDER THE SUN; GO AFTER THOSE WHO HAVE IT AND LEARN FROM THEM TO MAKE YOU ONE OF THEM! Ecclesiastes 1:7-11, 'All the rivers run into the sea; yet the sea is not full; unto the place from whence the rivers come, thither they return again. All things are full of labour; man cannot utter it: the eye is not satisfied with seeing, nor the ear filled with hearing. The thing that hath been, it is that which shall be; and that which is done is that which shall be done: and there is no new thing under the sun. Is there any thing whereof it may be said, See, this is new? it hath been already of old time, which was before us.'

THE NINE 'D's of DESTINY

These life-changing keys will make a tremendous impact on your life, career, business and ministry. I believe these principles must be the bedrock upon which major decisions are built. Every visionary or serious-minded, destiny-minded and purpose-driven individual, minister, businessman, entrepreneur or leader must prioritize and consider this in their choice of a marriage partner [if not married or about to remarry], choice of ministry, vocation, employees, employment, profession or career with the hindsight, sight, farsight and within the foresight of DESTINY.

DESTINY IS NOT DECIDED; DESTINY IS DISCOVERED!

DESTINY IS NOT WAITED ON; DESTINY IS PURSUED!

DESTINY IS VIGOROUSLY PURSUED UNTIL IT IS FULFILLED!

NINE 'D's THAT GUARANTEE DESTINY:

Philippians 3:12,
'Not as though I had already attained, either were already perfect: but I follow after, if that I may apprehend that for which also I am apprehended of Christ Jesus.'

Destiny must be fulfilled – that's all that matters!

1. DISCOVER YOUR DESTINY/ASSIGNMENT/ PURPOSE:

a. There is a predetermined counsel of God over your head.

b. Until you show up, no one can do what you are called to do.

c. You are created for a divine assignment.

d. Until you arrive on the scene, no one will sit down.

e. Until you arrive on the scene to deal with Goliath, everyone remains in fear.

f. Destiny is discovered, not decided by your parents.1 Peter 1:20, 'Who verily was foreordained before the foundation of the world, but was manifest in these last times for you,'

g. Your destiny was pre-ordained: Psalm 40:7, 'Then said I, Lo, I come: in the volume of the book it is written of me,'

Hebrews 10:7, 'Then said I, Lo, I come (in the volume of the book it is written of me,) to do thy will, O God.'

h. You are here to fulfil what is written of you in the volume of the book, so, find it and fulfil it. I have come to do what is written of me in the volume of the books [Volumes of stuff have been written of me for which I am here to accomplish].

i. Destiny is discovered, so discover your destiny – discover that destiny.

Why? There is a day of reckoning: On that day, Hebrews 9:27 says, 'And as it is appointed unto men once to die, but after this the judgment:' You will be asked, 'Did you discover and did you do; did you fulfill your assignment – not mine - yours?

j. You will know your assignment and understand your assignment by the volume of books: Daniel 9:2, 'In the first year of his reign I Daniel understood by books the number of the years, whereof the word of the LORD came to Jeremiah the prophet, that he would accomplish seventy years in the desolations of Jerusalem.'

QUESTION:
Once Assignment has been discovered, what's next?

2. DECIDE FOR YOUR DESTINY /ASSIGNMENT / PURPOSE:

Deuteronomy 2:24, 'Rise ye up, take your journey, and pass over the river Arnon: behold, I have given into thine hand Sihon the Amorite, king of Heshbon, and his land: begin to possess it, and contend with him in battle.'

a. Make a conscious decision to fulfill your assignment, no matter what!

b. It's one thing to discover it; it's another to consciously work at it and fulfill it. LIFE DOES NOT GIVE YOU WHAT YOU DESERVE: LIFE GIVES YOU ONLY WHAT YOU DEMAND!

c. Make a decision for destiny. Tick the box and vote for it. Say 'yes' every day to your assignment not 'yes' one time.

   - Paul said, 'I die daily' – i.e. I have decided.
   - Moses said, 'Whether it is convenient or inconvenient, I have heard God's voice; I am going to Egypt.'
   - Moses said again in Deuteronomy 30:19, '……. choose life that both thou and thy seed may live.'
   - Joshua said. '……..as for me and my house we will serve the Lord.'

d. Make a choice for destiny / the calling of God on your life.

e. **De-emphasize the things that don't matter and concentrate on the things that matter – destiny.**

f. **Major in on the majors and minor in on the minors.**

g. Be consumed with your assignment. Say with the psalmist, the zeal of the Lord has consumed me. Psalm 119:139, 'My zeal hath consumed me, because mine enemies have forgotten thy words.'

Say with Paul in 1 Corinthians 9:16, 'For though I preach the gospel, I have nothing to glory of: for necessity is laid upon me; yea, woe is unto me, if I preach not the gospel!'

h. Unseen forces back those who make a decision for destiny. Something decides to back a man who is facing the right direction.

i. Make a decision for what you have discovered, not partially, but absolutely - 100%. It's All or Nothing!

j. Be intoxicated with your assignment. Let it be the final arbiter based on God's purpose for your life for all decisions you make.

k. Be intoxicated with your destiny. Looking back turns people into pillars of salt. Bible says in Hebrews 10:39, 'But we are not of them who draw back unto perdition; but of them that believe to the saving of the soul.'

   - Say with Paul, 'I will run the race that is set before me.'
   - Say with Esther 'I will run the race that is set before me, and if I perish in so doing, I perish.'
   - Say with Joshua, 'Let us go up at once to possess the land for we are well able.'
   - Jesus said, 'I am offered up' and eventually said, 'It is finished.' – So, go up and finish your race.

3. DELIBERATELY CHART YOUR FUTURE/DESTINY:

LIFE DOES NOT GIVE YOU WHAT YOU DESERVE BUT WHAT YOU DEMAND. So, Take deliberate steps to fulfil destiny. (Deuteronomy 2:24; Matthew 11:12)

Jim Rohn said: "I used to say, 'I sure hope things will change;' then I learned that the only way things are going to change for me is when I change."

Every sustained, progressive, successful move or person and organisation has change as an obsession, addiction, a habit and behaviour.

Change is hard to live with but impossible to live without.

A leader says if it's going to be it's up to me.

Bernard Berenson said: "Would that I could stand on a busy corner, hats in hand and beg people to throw me all their wasted hours."

Thomas Edison said, "When I have finally decided that a matter is worth getting, I go ahead on it and to make trial after trial until it comes."

4. DETERMINE TO PURSUE DESTINY:

Joshua 3:5, 'And Joshua said unto the people, Sanctify

yourselves: for tomorrow the LORD will do wonders among you.'

Your sanctification [separation] today will determine your wonders tomorrow.

What you do today will determine what the Lord will do among you tomorrow.

Today is very crucial for tomorrow.

Martha Washington said, "I am still determined to be cheerful and happy in whatever situation I may be; for I have learned from experience that greater part of our happiness or misery depends upon our dispositions, and not upon our circumstances."

5. DEVELOP YOURSELF FOR YOUR DESTINY:

Develop yourself for your destiny through adequate, relevant knowledge and wisdom.

Wisdom is the ability to use your mind to make effective decisions. So, to be able to make effective decisions you need wisdom.

Proverbs 4:7-9 (Living Bible) reads, 'Determination to be wise is the first step to becoming wise and with wisdom develop common sense and good judgment; if you exalt wisdom, she will exalt you; hold fast and she will lead you to great honour, she will place a beautiful crown upon your head.'

Your success is linked with wisdom. The more informed you are, the better you are in your thinking. A well-informed person makes a better judgment in decision–making than a less-informed person.

The more you learn, the more your brains are exercised for productive ventures.

Those who do not think about the future cannot have one.

Whatever got you to where you are today is not enough to keep you there.

To earn more, you must learn more.

You can learn anything you need to learn in order to achieve any goal you set for yourself.

The more you learn the wiser you become. Paul said in 2 Timothy 2:15, 'Study to show thyself approved unto God, a workman that needeth not to be ashamed, rightly dividing the word of truth.'

Paul's exhortation in the above passage of scripture is not only applicable in the spiritual realm but in our careers, professions, vocations and in life in general. You need to study continuously to show yourself approved in every walk of life.

'The moment you stop learning, you stop leading.' – Rick Warren

Leaders are learners. Good leaders are hungry for learning, all the way to the grave.

'It's what you learn after you know it all that counts.' - John Wooden [NCAA Coach]

'Today a reader – tomorrow a leader.' - W. Fusselman

'Pay now, play later; play now, pay later.' - John Maxwell

'Leadership development is a lifetime journey – not a brief trip.' – John Maxwell

'As a rule….he (or she) who has the most information will have the greatest success in life.'
- Disraeli

We've all heard it before: knowledge is power. Because there is doubtless truth to this axiom, consume as much information as you possibly can, in a variety of subjects relevant to you and your work, career, profession, business, vocation or ministry. Success follows the person who brings something to the table when board meetings begin; they are well-read, well-informed and well-prepared. They never come across as ignorant in any subject.

6. DEDICATE OR DEVOTE YOURSELF TO YOUR DESTINY/ASSIGNMENT:

Determination alone is not enough; it must be backed by dedication to see manifestation.

a. **There is a difference between decision and dedication.**

b. **There is a difference between determination and dedication.**

c. **There is a difference between intention and dedication.**

d. Tie yourself to your destiny – that's what dedication means. Exodus 39:30, 'And they made the plate of the holy crown of pure gold, and wrote upon it a writing, like to the engravings of a signet, HOLINESS TO THE LORD.' i.e. Total Commitment to a divine cause

e. Dedicate your life – consecrate your life to your destiny.

f. Let it be uncompromising – don't compromise!

g. Be sold out to your assignment.

h. Free yourself from any excess baggage, i.e. weights. (Hebrews 12:1-2)

  - Your partner must not be or become a weight in your

pursuit of destiny and that is why you must first of all discover your purpose, i.e. why you are here and where you are going – are they heading in the same direction as you? If you don't choose well, they will slow you down, delay you, derail you and eventually destroy you.

i. Let your assignment totally consume you.

TIMELESS TRUTHS:

1. MINISTRY IS A DISCOVERY, A DECISION AND A DEDICATION!

2. DESTINY IS A DISCOVERY, A DECISION AND A DEDICATION!

3. ASSIGNMENT IN LIFE IS A DISCOVERY, A DECISION AND A DEDICATION!

4. **Time is a privilege - maximize it.**

5. **Long life is fulfillment within time allocated.**

6. **Success is fulfilling assignment within time allocated.**

7. **Wasted time is like a haemorrhaging assignment.**

8. **Making the most of your time is making the most of your life, destiny, purpose, assignment, ministry**

or career!

9. **Wasting the most of your time is wasting the most of your life, destiny, purpose, assignment, ministry or career – you choose!**

10. **Destiny comes to a total collapse or halt when time is wasted on irrelevant things and irrelevant people.**

11. **Dedicate your heart, soul, thoughts, money, resources, time, finances, energies, sitting, standing, walking, running, intellect, income, speech, conversation, strengths, investments, everything, on the fulfillment of your assignment.**
    Join the psalmist and pray always, Psalm 90:12, 'So teach us to number our days, that we may apply our hearts unto wisdom.'

j. Be addicted to priority-management, not just time-management.

k. Ministry, business and career success is not a coincidence.

l. There is no 'plan B' or middle ground – all my eggs are in one basket. As a wise person said, 'Put all your eggs in one basket and watch it grow and reproduce and expand and impact nations.'

m. Focus on the assignment: Refuse to be distracted, keep

your gaze on the promises and not the problems. Be like a postage stamp; stick to one thing till you finish it.

n.   Let the fabric of your life be intoxicated with the vision. (Habakkuk 2:2)

o.   Differentiate between career assignment and personal one. (**Luke 16:12**)

p.   Be informed adequately and appropriately for your assignment. To be informed is to be transformed; to be uninformed is to be deformed.

q.   Appraise the vision regularly and make the vision practical and applicable. Concrete choices are easy to keep.

r.   Stay motivated: It will make you follow your vision doggedly in the face of challenges and difficulty. Do not wait for others to motivate you. Joshua and Caleb were highly motivated and so was Paul, Daniel and the three Hebrew boys. (Deuteronomy 31:27-30; Numbers 13:30; Romans 8:30-39; Daniel 1; 3; 6)

s.   Appreciate and Command yourself. (Matthew 25:34-40)
     - Give yourself rewards for effort, results and accomplishments.

t.   Think of possibilities and not obstacles. (Mark 9:23; Matthew 19:26)

u.   Have a good self-support system [ego and confidence].

(Philippians 4:13)
- Take examples from achievers. (Hebrews 12:1)
- REMEMBER: The covenant must be perpetuated.

7. DILIGENTLY PURSUE YOUR DESTINY:

It was Victor Hugo who said, "He who every morning plans the transactions of the day and follows out the plan, carries a thread that will guide him through the labyrinth of the most busy life."

WHAT YOU HAVE IS JUST ENOUGH. MAKE USE OF IT AND DEVELOP YOURSELF FOR YOUR DESTINATION.

"You don't sleep with vision, you run with vision." - Bishop David Oyedepo

"Everything depends on execution, having just a vision is no solution." - Stephen Sondheim

"A man is a success if he gets up in the morning and gets to bed at night, and in between he does what he wants to do." - Bob Dyan

"I do not believe in a fate that falls on men however they act, but I do believe in a fate that falls on men unless they act." - G. K. Chesterton

"A winner is someone who recognizes his talent, works his

tail off to develop them into skills and uses these skills to accomplish his goals." - Larry Bird

"The big challenge is to become all that you have the possibility of becoming. You cannot believe what it does to the human spirit to maximize your human potential and stretch your self to the limit." - Jim Rohn

DILIGENCE: "Seest thou a man diligent in his business? He shall stand before kings; He shall not stand before mean men." (KJV)

"Do you know a hard-working man? He shall be successful and stand before kings." (LBT) - Proverbs 22:29

"The right to be heard does not automatically mean the right to be taken seriously." - Humphrey Hubert

"Originality and the feeling of one's own dignity are achieved through work and struggle."- Fyodor Dostoyevsky

"Nothing comes easily, work hard! Face the challenge! You certainly will succeed." - Oti Orie

"It is said that one machine can do the work of 50 ordinary men. No machine however can do the work of one extraordinary man." - Tehyi Hsteh
(Lesson: Be the best at what you do)

"The reason why worry kills more people than work is that more people worry than work." - Robert Frost

"My father taught me to do more than you get paid for as an investment in your future." - Jim Rohn

Lesson: (Read more, learn more, give more. Go the extra mile without being asked or told to - do all this 'carry-forward')

"He who labours diligently need never despair; for all things are accomplished by diligence and labour." - Meneder

8. DISCIPLINE YOURSELF FOR YOUR DESTINY:

"When wealth is lost, nothing is lost; when health is lost, something is lost; when character is lost, all is lost."
- Billy Graham

"Ability may get you to the top, but it takes character to keep you there." - John Wooden, NCAA coach

"The foundation stones for a balanced success are honesty, character, integrity, faith, love and loyalty." - Zig Ziglar

Conduct versus character: conduct is what you display on the outside for all to see while character is who and what you really are on the inside which only you know. It was John Wooden, NCAA coach who said: 'Be more concerned with your character than with your reputation. Your character is what you really are while your reputation is merely what others think you are.'

REMEMBER: He who chooses the beginning of a road,

also chooses its outcome.

Ecclesiastes 10:1, 'Dead flies cause the ointment of the apothecary to send forth a stinking savour: so doth a little folly him that is in reputation for wisdom and honour.'

'As Dead flies putrifies the perfumers ointment and cause it to give off a foul odour so does a little folly to one respected for wisdom and honour.'

If one dead fly falls into that nice smelling odour, it putrifies. Because it decomposes, it changes the chemical structure of the oil and everything starts smelling bad.

Lesson: Only one dead fly can make something that was destined to smell sweet to now smell with a foul odour I.e. a little folly, a little foolishness can destroy the destiny of one who was destined to be very wise. Our bad habits can derail our greatness. I don't know what dead flies have landed on your perfume; some are destined to be perfumes but are smelling like dead flies because of one little folly or one bad company or the friends they associate with, move with, seek counsel or advice from. (Read Proverbs 22:24-28; Psalm 1:1-3; 1 Corinthians 15:33)

One wise move can make a genius out of a dummy while one reckless move can make a dummy out of one who was destined to be a genius. Discipline yourself! Private homework averts public scandals.

'Discipline is the soul of an army: it makes small numbers formidable, procures success to the weak and confers esteem on [brings esteem to] all.' - George Washington

Read more on discipline and indiscipline in chapter ten of this book.

9. DIE OR BE WILLING TO DIE FOR YOUR DESTINY/ASSIGNMENT

a. Be totally committed to your assignment.
    - Noah was committed to the ark irrespective; the three Hebrew boys were committed irrespective of the fire; Daniel was committed – I will pray irrespective of the lion – **DIE FOR WHAT YOU LIVE FOR!**

b. Is there anything you are willing to die for? If not, that is not really your assignment. YOUR ASSIGNMENT WILL CONSUME YOU!

c. Whatever is not worth dying for is not worth living for.

d. Death is the door to life. John 12:24-25 says, 'Verily, verily, I say unto you, Except a corn of wheat fall into the ground and die, it abideth alone: but if it die, it bringeth forth much fruit. He that loveth his life shall lose it; and he that hateth his life in this world shall keep it unto life eternal.'

e. Once you decide, 'I can die for this assignment', fear

goes out of the door.

f.   Real life emanates out of death.

g.   Until you die, you can't live.

h.   Until you go down, you can never go up. Ephesians 4:10, 'He that descended is the same also that ascended up far above all heavens, that he might fill all things.'

Philippians 2:5-11, 'Let this mind be in you, which was also in Christ Jesus: Who, being in the form of God, thought it not robbery to be equal with God: But made himself of no reputation, and took upon him the form of a servant, and was made in the likeness of men: And being found in fashion as a man, he humbled himself, and became obedient unto death, even the death of the cross. Wherefore God also hath highly exalted him, and given him a name which is above every name: That at the name of Jesus every knee should bow, of things in heaven, and things in earth, and things under the earth; And that every tongue should confess that Jesus Christ is Lord, to the glory of God the Father.'

[For more information on fulfilling destiny, order my books: What is Ministry; Generating Finances for Ministry; How to Negotiate your desired future with today's currency; Leadership Secrets; Leadership Nuggets; Leadership Capsules; DESTINY BLOCKERS Vs. DESTINY-MAKERS and 200 Questions you must ask, investigate and know before you say, 'I DO' from www.houseofjudah.org.uk]

Welcome to the best season of your life!

FENCE-BUILDERS

ADVICE:

1. Don't start dancing before the band starts playing.

2. It is better to build a fence on top of a cliff than a hospital at the bottom of a cliff.

3. Prevention is better than cure.

4. It is better to try to keep a bad thing from happening than it is to fix the bad thing once it has happened.

5. An ounce of prevention is better than a pound of cure.

6. If we spend more money on education, so that children learn to be responsible citizens, we won't have to spend so much money on prisons. Why? Prevention is better than cure.

7. It is better to stop something bad happening than it is to deal with it after it has happened. More advice is needed on how to stay healthy to prevent needless casualties.

8. Taking care of your teeth through good hygiene and regular dental care is better than having to replace your natural teeth at $1,000 a pop.

9. An ounce of prevention is worth a pound of cure.

10. It's more prudent to head off a disaster beforehand than to deal with it after it occurs. The proverb has been traced back to 'De Legibus' (c. 1240) by English Jurist Henry De Bracton (d. 1268). First attested in the United States in "Documentary History of Maine Containing Baxter Manuscripts ..." From "Random House Dictionary of Popular Proverbs and Sayings" by Gregory Y. Titelman. Another reference dates the idea back to the Roman poet Persius (A.D.c 58), "Meet the malady on its way." The first English version, "Prevention is so much better than healing because it saves the labor of being sick," Thomas Adams's "Works" 1630. The English Satirist Thomas C. Haliburton repeated the current version in "The Clockmaker" or "The Sayings and Doings of Samuel Slick of Slickville," 1837. From "Wise Words and Wives' Tales: The Origins, Meanings and Time-Honored Wisdom of Proverbs and Folk Sayings Olde and New" by Stuart Flexner and Doris Flexner (Avon Books, New York, 1993). Page 144.

Another way of saying it - a stitch in time saves nine.

http://www.phrases.org.uk/meanings/a-stitch-in-time.html
Or as Barney Fife would say - nip it in the bud.

Barney Fife: Well, today's eight-year-olds are tomorrow's teenagers. I say this calls for action and now. Nip it in the bud. First sign of youngsters going wrong, you've got to nip it in the bud.

From the Phrase Finder

NO RINGY, NO DINGY!

UNTIL YOU ARE READY, LET LOVE SLEEP!

UNTIL YOU ARE FULLY AND LEGALLY READY, LET CERTAIN PASSIONS REST!

UNTIL YOU ARE READY, LET LOVE SLEEP AND FRIENDSHIP AWAKEN!! As the saying goes: LET SLEEPING DOGS LIE!

Songs 2:7, 'I charge you, O ye daughters of Jerusalem, by the roes, and by the hinds of the field, that ye stir not up, nor awake my love, till he please.'

Don't light certain fires before its appropriate time. Proverbs 6:27-28 'Can a man take fire in his bosom, and his clothes not be burned? Can one go upon hot coals, and his feet not be burned?'

If you break the hedge the serpent will bite you: Ecclesiastes 10:8-9, 'He that diggeth a pit shall fall into it; and whoso breaketh an hedge, a serpent shall bite him. Whoso removeth stones shall be hurt therewith; and he that cleaveth wood shall be endangered thereby.'

"Control your destiny or someone else will." - Jack Welch, CEO General Electric Company

Chapter
Three

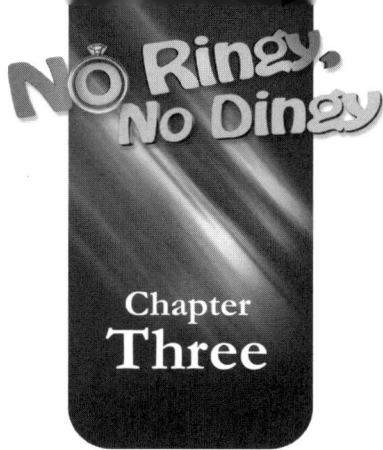

FORGET THE PAST AND PRESS ON!

Keys to forgetting/overcoming the past and becoming all you were born to be:

"We will remember not the words of our enemies, but the silence of our friends."
- Martin Luther King Jr.

Evil is perpetuated not because of the strength and power of evil but more because of the silence of good men.

"There is no easy walk to freedom anywhere."
- Nelson Mandela

"Everyone has a past; but never allow your past to get in the way of your future."
- Michael Hutton-Wood

"Darkness cannot drive out darkness; only light can; hate cannot drive out hate; only love can do that."
- Martin Luther King Jr.

A newborn baby has no past. You've been given a second chance; seize it and maximize it.

There are a lot of regrets, disappointments, failures, mistakes, betrayals, let-downs, humiliations and other acts that have caused all of us a lot of grief in the past including relationships. Dwelling on them to plague us with guilt, unforgiveness, bitterness, hatred, animosity, resentment, restlessness, being mean and plotting to seek revenge which are all possibilities that come to mind is not the answer; but learning valuable lessons from them, moving on, using them to our advantage by letting the new possibilities we create supersede our past is.

So the question is: What drives your life - your past, your present or your future? YOUR LIFE IS EITHER DRIVEN BY YOUR PAST, YOUR PRESENT OR YOUR FUTURE.

Let me begin by sharing with you some secrets you need to know about your past, your present and your future. Many people are driven by the guilt of their past. They spend their entire lives running from regrets and hiding from their shame. Guilt-driven people are manipulated by their memories. **They allow their past to control their future. They often unconsciously punish themselves by sabotaging their** own success.

THE FUTURE VERSUS THE PAST

"Your past is important, but it is not nearly as important to your present as is the way you see your future."
- Dr. Tony Campolo

Regardless of your past, your future is a clean slate.

"If things go wrong, don't go with them."
- Roger Babson

From the book, 'Buy The Future' written by Dr. Mensa Otabil, we discover the following:

'There are three realities of time – past, present and the future. The past and the future occur in the mind. The past is a memory. The future is an imagination. These two expressions of time occur in the mind. The reality of the past is in our memories of what has already happened. The reality of the future is in how we imagine things will happen. The past is very powerful because it is the only expression of time that has already happened and therefore the only one which imprints itself on our minds.

The present is reality that is still unfolding, as such, it can be observed and appreciated. The future on the other hand has not happened. So it has no reference point. Most people's lives consist of their memories of the past and their observation of the present. Such people respond only to what has happened and what is happening. They are reactive to life's choices and not proactive. They feel powerless to change what they don't like in their own lives and often lack the courage to question their choices.'

"Those who cannot remember the past are condemned to repeat it."
- George Santanya

Santanya argued that **knowledge gained from the past must be used to avoid repetition of the same mistakes.** Rightly so! **We are products of our past but we don't have to be controlled by our past.** Learn from the past but don't be controlled by it. **When given the choice between the past and future, always choose the future over the past.**

WE ARE PRODUCTS OF OUR PAST, BUT WE DON'T HAVE TO BE PRISONERS OF IT.

1. Everyone has a past that they are either proud of or regret.

2. You are not the only one who has a past you are not proud of - the question is, 'What are you going to do about it?'

3. It's your past - that was then - this is now!

4. It's in your past; learn from it and move on.

5. The past is your experience; the present is your opportunity and the future is your friend on condition that you embrace the opportunities of today to create your desired future.

6. Use the past to your advantage:
- Use the past to invent an enviable future.
- Don't get bitter - get better!
- Gain some light - insight about your enviable future.

7. Take the bricks thrown at you in your past to lay a solid foundation for your future. Look at it this way: at least you don't have to visit the builders' merchants to buy those bricks - they threw them at you free of charge.

8. Don't allow your past to control your future - you will be sabotaging your own destiny.

9. Stop spending your entire life running from regrets and hiding your shame.

10. God's purpose is never limited by your past.

11. God specializes in giving people a fresh start.

12. Your past is irrelevant and inconsequential when your season for fulfilling destiny arrives, if only you learn from it; believe this truth and move on.

13. You are only hurting yourself by dwelling on your bitter past. For your own sake learn from it and let it go.

14. The best way to deal with and forget what you don't like about your past is to produce something new.

15. The best way to deal with and forget what you don't like about your past is to produce i.e. become fruitful and productive in one way or the other; keep yourself occupied and challenged by new opportunities to be productive.

16. Be engaged in an activity of some sort - a venture that you enjoy which produces to your satisfaction and adds value both to you and others. It will occupy your mind and supersede i.e. make you forget the pain, bitterness, failure and humiliation of the past.

17. When you are fruitful / productive, you will forget the past.

18. The way to deal with memories you do not like is to produce what you like.

19. The way to forget the toil, bitterness, memories of your past is to have an experience that supersedes your past memory. That superseding experience will make your past memories and experience insignificant.

20. Control your past – "He who controls the past controls the future."
– George Orwell, 1984

21. Learn from the past by all means but like the Apostle

Paul, Forget the past and press on - move on. Paul said:
1. Forgetting the past
2. I press on
3. Reaching for the prize………
TREND: FORGET THE PAST, PRESS ON, REACH FOR……….

22. You can't change yesterday - you can maximize today.

23. Release yesterday i.e. release the pain and shame of yesterday and live in the power of today.

24. Resentment hurts you more than the person you resent.

25. Forgiveness is more for your benefit than the one you forgive. Forgiveness is mandatory but relationship is optional - so forgive.

26. Those who have hurt you in the past cannot continue to hurt you unless you hold on to the pain through resentment. Your past is your past - nothing will change it; but you can make something extraordinary out of your present for your desired future.

27. The future is visualized by learning from, forgetting [getting over] and refusing to be controlled by bad history.

28. LEARN and ACT ON LESSONS FROM HISTORY:

"Life is lived forward but understood backward."
- Dei Tumi, motivational speaker

"There is no reason to repeat bad history."
- Eleanor Holmes Norton, American lawyer and civil rights leader

29. "History is the discovering of the constant and universal principles of human nature."
- David Hume

30. "A GENERATION THAT IGNORES HISTORY HAS NO PAST AND HAS NO FUTURE."
- ROBERT HEINLEIN

Chapter
Four

YOUR CHOICES AND YOUR FUTURE!

60 KEYS TO DESIGNING YOUR FUTURE

1. 'We all have two choices. We can make a living or we can design a life.' – Jim Rohn

2. WRONG CHOICES LEAD TO BAD DECISIONS WHILST RIGHT CHOICES LEAD TO GOOD DECISIONS!

3. SUCCESS IS BY CHOICE AND FAILURE IS BY CHOICE! You choose!

4. Everything you do involves a choice between what is more important and what is less important. Choose well. You are where you are and what you are because of yourself - your own choices and decisions.

5. **Every choice has an end result!**

6. **'We are free up to the point of choice, then, the choice controls the chooser.' - Mary Crowley**

7. **"Control your destiny or someone else will." - Jack Welch,** CEO, General Electric Company

8. **When it comes to destiny - Friendship is not by force – it's by choice!**

9. **'Our greatest power is the power to choose. The thoughts we have chosen have brought us where we are today. Our thoughts today will bring us where we will be tomorrow.' - Dr. Myles Munroe**

10. **He who chooses the beginning of a road also chooses its outcome.**

11. '.........Choose you this day whom you will serve .... but as for me and my house we will serve the Lord.' - Joshua (Joshua 24:15)

12. You can choose to become extraordinary or remain ordinary. It's your choice! Refuse to be ordinary or to remain ordinary.

13. **"Self-discipline is the ability to make yourself do what you should do, when you should do it, whether you feel like it or not." - Elbert Hubbard,** author and lecturer

14. Extraordinary people are ordinary people who decided to do something extra that the ordinary people were not willing to do. So they are ordinary people who paid the extra price required.

15. "Sometimes you must fight and win, just because all the pain and suffering you experienced up to that point on your quest, would be rendered futile if you were to surrender now." - Alvin Day

16. The mouth is not meant to describe our problems, but to prescribe our solutions!

17. 'Chase your passion, not your pension.' – Denis Waitley

18. Success that is not prepared for can destroy a man!

19. At the root of everything outstanding is understanding! So, get understanding.

20. **You cannot have what you speak against!**

21. **You must use time as a tool, not a couch! - John F. Kennedy**

22. 'Master communication and you manage conflict.' - King Solomon

23. What you are ready to give up today for tomorrow will determine what you can have and walk in tomorrow!

24. Live today with tomorrow in mind by sacrificing your present for your future. That is how you secure an envious future.

25. Successful people are path-finders, trail-blazers, pace-setters and chart new courses. Start now!

26. Your future is determined by your daily choices and decisions.

27. The future is determined by your daily schedule; tell me what you do every day and I'll tell you what kind of future you are likely to have.

28. The future is created by people who don't walk in circles where they are tolerated but in circles where they are celebrated.

29. Those who do not think about the future cannot have one.

30. The future is created by those who have taken the bricks thrown at them to lay a solid foundation for the release, maximization and fulfilment of their destiny.

31. 'The best way to predict the future is to invent it.' - Alan Kay

32. The future is what you anticipate, plan for and work at to create. You expect it and diligently pursue it. The future is what you create.

33. The future is not hoped for - it is smartly sweated for.

34. The future is certain when adequate preparation meets with opportunity.

35. The future is not for those who intend to have it but those who work at having it; because nothing was ever achieved by intention alone.

36. The future is what you look up to, not what you look down on.

37. The future is what you buy, not what you sell. BUY THE FUTURE!

38. The future is created by those who even though they might be in the gutter now can still see and focus their eyes on the stars.

39. The future is created by knowledge, not ignorance. It is created through acquisition and application of adequate, relevant knowledge, wisdom and understanding, not negligence and dereliction of duty.

40. The future is created by those who build with generations in mind.

41. The future must be dusted daily and picked up, not shelved.

42. The future must be consciously worked at and vigorously pursued.

43. The future must be planned for, prepared for and relentlessly pursued until it is accomplished.

44. The future must discipline you and be set before your eyes daily.

45. The future is created by the full productive deployment and use of one's mental faculties – the mind.

QUOTES ON THE MIND:
a. The mind can be described as putting your brain to work.
b. You cannot become a head until you put your head to work.
c. Those who use their heads cannot end up as tails.
d. If you find yourself as a tail the only thing to do is start using your head. It is your head that puts you ahead.
e. Every slave remains in slavery until he begins to put his head to work - use his head. The cheapest way to terminate slavery and begging is to put your head to work. Use your head - use your brain. Sonship does not guarantee you automatic rulership. You have to be a son with a brain at work. (Proverbs 11:29; 17:2)

46. The future is created and arrived at by diligent [hard and smart] workers, not lazy people. There is no future for a lazy man. ONLY HARD WORKERS END UP AS HIGH FLIERS!

47. The future is created by those who instead of celebrating their abundance, rather save up and take advantage of new

investment opportunities that present themselves.

48. The future is purposely created by people who don't wait for abundance but create abundance. As the saying goes, 'If you wait, you waste.'

49. The future must be embraced, not shunned. It must be believed and acted on to be realized.

50. The future is created by those who don't tolerate and can't stand to hear the words, 'It can't be done.'

51. The future must drive you, not drag you. Your destiny must be a drug that intoxicates you, not a drag.

52. The future must intoxicate you to action, not put you to sleep. It must determine how long you sleep.

53. The future is created by those who are effective not just busy – being busy should never be confused with being effective in life.

54. The future is created by those who are moving progressively forward, not just being in motion – **just being in motion does not necessarily mean you are moving forward**. People going everywhere never arrive anywhere in particular!

55. The future is created by those whose lives are not lived just to conform but to transform, add value and revolutionize.

56. The future is created by those who invest and double the worth of their money.

57. The future must determine what you do, what you say, where you go, what calls you make, what conversations you engage in, your associations and what you give your attention to.

58. The future must determine your priorities – the what, who, where, why, when, how and which. DON'T BE JUST A TIME-MANAGER BUT A PRIORITY-MANAGER! Prioritize!

59. The future must be arrived at, at all cost by right means. Success by all means holds no future; only success by right means does!

60. The future is arrived at by paying the right price; the required price. A price must be paid for an expected future – the required price.

Having discovered the power and relevance of our choices on our future, let's now examine why you must make a choice for abstinence.

Chapter
Five

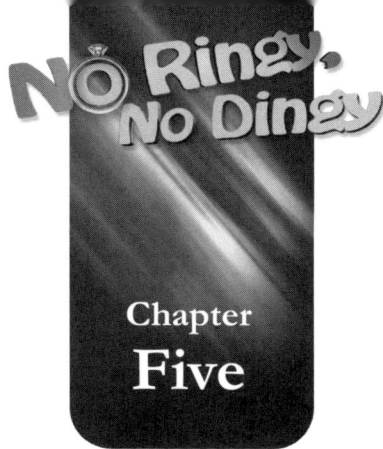

WHY ABSTINENCE?

"Abstain from all appearance of evil. And the very God of peace sanctify you wholly; and I pray God your whole spirit and soul and body be preserved blameless unto the coming of our Lord Jesus Christ. Faithful is he that calleth you, who also will do it**." - 1 Thessalonians 5:22-24**

"Know ye not that ye are the temple of God, and that the Spirit of God dwelleth in you?" - **1 Corinthians 3:16-20**

"Know ye not that he which is joined to an harlot is one body? for two, saith he, shall be one flesh. But he that is joined unto the Lord is one spirit. Flee fornication. Every sin that a man doeth is without the body; but he that committeth fornication sinneth against his own body. What? know ye not that your body is the temple of the Holy Ghost which is in you, which ye have of God, and ye are not your own? For ye are bought with a price: therefore glorify God in your body, and in your spirit, which are God's." - **1 Corinthians 6:16-20**

What is the definition of Abstinence?

Abstinence (Ab-sti-nence) is defined as a positive lifestyle for an adolescent that promotes self-control, character, discipline, dedication, devotion and a solid foundation for lasting friendships and for committed love within the context of preparation for marriage.

Abstinence is the commitment to not participate in sexual activity, which may include intercourse, genital contact, or other sexually arousing activities and behaviours.

Abstinence is not having sex. A person who decides to practice abstinence has decided not to have sex.

Why Abstinence?

If two people don't have sex, then sperm can't fertilize an egg and there's no possibility of a pregnancy. Some forms of birth control depend on barriers that prevent the sperm from reaching the egg (such as condoms or diaphragms). Others interfere with the menstrual cycle (as birth control pills do). With abstinence, no barriers or pills are necessary because the person is not having sex.

How Reliable is Abstinence?

Abstinence is 100% effective in preventing pregnancy. Although many birth control methods can have high rates of success if used properly, they can fail occasionally. Practicing abstinence ensures that a girl won't become pregnant because there's no opportunity for sperm to fertilize an egg.

Abstinence is a very important part of life. The purpose of this book is to explain what abstinence is, why abstinence, benefits of abstinence, teach you how to discover and fulfil your purpose, why you must forget the past, choose life, prioritise, make the right choice of a marriage partner by positioning yourself to resist and overcome temptation and fulfil your destiny (why you are here).

BENEFITS OF ABSTINENCE:

1. The first reason and probably the most important is to please your Maker so He makes your life pleasurable (Job 36:11). As a Christian and believer, you are supposed to wait until marriage because it is a sin to practice premarital sex. Ecclesiastes 10:8-9, 'He that diggeth a pit shall fall into it; and whoso breaketh an hedge, a serpent shall bite him. Whoso removeth stones shall be hurt therewith; and he that cleaveth wood shall be endangered thereby.'

2. Your body does not belong to you - it belongs to your Maker.

3. Your body is one of your greatest assets on earth to enable you fulfil your predestined purpose on earth. Without it, you cannot fulfil destiny.

4. Aids discovery and pursuit of purpose.

5. Helps you fulfil destiny.

6. Prevents guilt.

7. Prevents shame.

8. Prevents delays to destiny-fulfilment.

9. Prevents derailment to destiny-fulfilment.

10. Aids realisation of set goals.

11. Helps you complete your education within the prescribed time in style and with dignity.

12. Helps you maintain your virginity and dignity before marriage.

13. Helps you keep yourself for both your destiny and future partner.

14. Brings you positive pride.

15. Is a major achievement.

16. Aids preservation of your health and life from unwanted pregnancy, disgrace, shame and calamity.

17. Prevents needless frustration.

18. No excess baggage to carry.

19. Aids focus on your assignment in life.

20. Takes the stress of the unwanted from your life.

21. Helps you live a meaningful life.

22. Helps you avoid unwanted pregnancy. Even though contraceptives can aid the undisciplined in the process, however, abstinence is the only one hundred percent positive way to prevent pregnancy.

23. You avoid STD's. The only sure way to one hundred percent prevention of sexually transmitted diseases is total abstinence. Remember: you can contract sexually transmitted diseases from other sexual acts as well.

24. You reduce or eliminate the risk of infertility. Some sexually transmitted diseases can cause infertility so that you can't have children in the future and even cancer.

25. Eliminates the spread of STD's. If everyone waited until they got married it would actually slow the spread of sexually transmitted diseases. It makes a lot of sense if you think about

it if two people wait until they get married then obviously neither one of them have an STD so they won't be passing it on. Even if one person in the relationship contracted an STD and the other waited until marriage, the STD would only be passed to one person if they stayed faithful, instead of a bunch of other people; however this must be a no-go area. The more people that practice abstinence, the better for society. Make a difference!

26. It is a booster for a happy, loving, peaceful, satisfied, fulfilled and more healthy and settled relationship.

27. There is more trust, less emotional baggage, and more respect. If someone respects themselves and their morals they attract more respect in return.

28. Studies have shown that when people practice abstinence they are happier as adults, more focussed, more productive, more successful, more impactful, more influential, more fulfilling and more financially successful as well.

29. Eliminates premature destruction of destinies.

30. Avoidance of stress and pressure on relationships caused by unnecessary arguments and disagreements.

31. Can ultimately save potentially healthy and strong relationships.

32. Abstinence can also provide a deeper connection and

deeper commitment with the person you are with and create a better relationship. Knowledge of a person's history of commitment to abstinence builds trust and allegiance.

33. One of the most important reasons for practicing abstinence is that it makes you fulfilled.

34. It prevents embarrassments, shame and disgrace.

35. So you will remember your Creator in the days of your youth. (Ecclesiastes 11:9; 12:1)

36. So you maximise your youthful days enjoying every aspect of it. You can only be physically young once. Enjoy it while you can. The glory of the youth is in their strength. Proverbs 20:29, 'The glory of young men is their strength: and the beauty of old men is the gray head.'

37. Enhances self-esteem through a discovery of purpose, discovery of gifts, discovery of strengths and opportunities and building skills such as positive goal-setting, decision-making, problem-solving, negotiation and refusal techniques to fulfil destiny in a grand style.

38. Waiting brings invaluable rewards both in the present and for the future.

Isaiah 40:31, 'But they that wait upon the Lord shall renew their strength; they shall mount up with wings as eagles; they shall run, and not be weary; and they shall walk, and not faint.'

Habakkuk 2:3, 'For the vision is yet for an appointed time, but at the end it shall speak, and not lie: though it tarry, wait for it; because it will surely come, it will not tarry.'

39. Abstinence makes one bold, confident, strong and courageous. (Joshua 1)

40. Empowers you to accomplish as many of your goals and dreams with no child to take care of. Lay aside every weight. (Hebrews 12:1-2)

Abstinence is not necessarily an easy choice to make and usually not an easy decision to stick with but with destiny in mind you must make the right choice which ultimately leads to good decisions whereas bad choices lead to wrong decisions.

Why is abstinence education so important?

Abstinence has as its exclusive purpose:

1. To enlighten, educate and illuminate youngsters that there are social, emotional, physical, educational, mental, psychological and health gains to be realized by abstaining from sexual activity prematurely.

2. To explain that abstinence from sexual activity outside marriage is the expected standard for all school-age, college-age children and university-age young adults.

3. That it is the only certain way to avoid out-of-wedlock pregnancy, sexually transmitted diseases and other associated health problems.

4. A mutually faithful monogamous relationship in the context of marriage is the expected standard of human sexual activity.

5. That sexual activity outside of the context of marriage is likely to have harmful psychological and physical effects.

6. That bearing children out-of-wedlock is likely to have harmful consequences for the child, the child's parents and society.

7. Teaching young people how to reject sexual advances and how alcohol and drug use increases vulnerability to sexual advances, hence the next chapter on how to avoid, resist and overcome temptations.

8. Teaching the importance of attaining self-sufficiency before engaging in sexual activity. God gave Adam his purpose, assignment in life, placed him in the appointed environment and gave him a job before He gave him a wife. Don't light certain fires before its appropriate time. Proverbs 6:27-28, 'Can a man take fire in his bosom, and his clothes not be burned? Can one go upon hot coals, and his feet not be burned?'

If you break the hedge, the serpent will bite you: Ecclesiastes 10:8-9, 'He that diggeth a pit shall fall into it; and whoso breaketh an hedge, a serpent shall bite him. Whoso removeth stones shall be hurt therewith; and he that cleaveth wood shall be endangered thereby.'

9. Abstinence education enhances decision-making and problem-solving skills while building self-confidence.

10. A coordinated approach to reducing teen sexual activity reduces public costs and improves the future for our youth.

11. Helps you enjoy and maximise fully your childhood, teenage, young and young adulthood years and grow from those vital stages into manhood and womanhood before taking care of another child. Proverbs 20:29, 'The glory of young men is their strength: and the beauty of old men is the gray head.'

12. Your future partner/spouse respects you immensely for disciplining yourself to wait for them.

13. Maintaining your virginity is an achievement. Entering marriage as a virgin is worthy of more than a Nobel peace prize.

14. You are a true and great example to your children for them to emulate in the future.

15. You have a clear conscience.

16. Is one of the smartest decisions you can ever make.

17. No worries about contracting an STD.

18. It enables you pursue your career without any excess baggage because you consciously rid your life of distractions and distracters.

19. It enables you plan and pursue your future unhindered by triviality.

20. It prevents unnecessary jealousies and envies that eat up many people's destinies.

21. Avoiding the pain of not being able to be pregnant when it really matters.

In response to the advice: 'DON'T JUST TELL PEOPLE TO STOP DOING WHAT IS WRONG; RATHER SHOW THEM HOW', in the next chapter, we will examine how to avoid, resist and overcome temptation so you don't become a statistic among previous casualties but rather are empowered to pursue destiny, heading eventually to making the right choice of a marriage partner in fulfilment of your ultimate purpose.

AVOIDING, RESISTING AND OVERCOMING TEMPTATION

WHAT TO KNOW AND DO IN THE TIMES OF TEMPTATIONS, TESTS AND TRIALS:

1 Corinthians 10:13, 'There hath no temptation taken you but such as is common to man: but God is faithful, who will not suffer you to be tempted above that ye are able; but will with the temptation also make a way to escape, that ye may be able to bear it.'

Having made a decision for abstinence and destiny, this chapter is for those who are very serious about overcoming every temptation they face! Scripture says in 2 Corinthians 2:14, 'Thanks be to God who causes us to triumph always.'

This is your victorious and triumphant chapter. The good news is: God will not suffer or allow you to be tempted above what you are able because He is faithful and **He will with every temptation you face make a way of escape for you that you will be able to bear it and overcome it.**

How To Overcome Every Temptation

Facts about Temptation:

1. Temptation is real.

2. Temptations will come.

3. Nobody is above temptation.

4. Everyone will be tempted.

5. Temptation is on the way.

6. No one can make you do what you don't want to do if you really don't want to.

7. Your desire to fulfil your goals in life is not temptation-proof.

8. As long as you are on this earth you will be tempted.

9. Nobody is under obligation not to tempt you.

10. **Nobody is under obligation not to tempt you - you are under obligation not to yield to temptation or place yourself in environments where you can be tempted to yield to it.** Because the Bible says offences will come, offences must of necessity come - temptations will come.

11. No one in his right mind will desire to fornicate or commit adultery or cheat people or be a crook to delay or derail their destiny. **So, your determination as a man to live a holy life and not to yield to temptation from women or vice versa is not dependent on the good behaviour of the women or the opposite sex - that's your responsibility.**

12. It's not based on the fact that you are in a church where all the women are disciplined, will not roll their eyes at you, try to catch your attention, not be interested in you, not wear miniskirts, display provocative gestures, show their legs, breasts, want you for themselves, not dress in a sensual or sexual way, etc. Some will.

13. So, your determination is not based on them; it's based within your own conviction. We must take full responsibility with a firm decision that even though we walk through a room or at a beach full of naked women or handsome men, we will not yield to temptation. We will still be what we have desired to be and not do what we must not do.

That should be our responsibility. For a man or a leader to say, 'I yielded because the women were tempting me' reveals your ignorance, lack of self control and your indiscipline.

Their responsibility as females is to look good and try to get the attention of men. So, even as a leader you are handsome, you occupy a position of power, influence, leadership and impact which many women admire and desire to have. It's natural - so you can't help it.

In life, people will be attracted to you, both male and female. If you are a man in a position of authority or responsibility, some ladies may wish they were your wife; that's their sincere wish; that's an honest desire and for most, that's not because they want you to fall or to destroy you; no, it's just because they like and admire you and desire to have someone like you. You are an embodiment or epitome of their ideal husband. If you were not taken, they would have desired or wouldn't mind having you as theirs - that's an honest DESIRE.

With all that said however, your determination to follow and pursue your vision as an individual or leader should not be based on them. Your determination to fulfil your assignment in life should be your focus. So your reaction to these advances should not be based on their looks, their provocations, advances, winks, smiles, hugs, praises, tears, phone calls, gifts, texts, volunteering to serve you, suggestive comments and indirect passes or their actions, desires, reactions, behaviour, morality, immorality, etc. It should be based on your personal responsibility to what you have decided and declared with your mouth about your priorities.

That means, you and I are responsible for disciplining our flesh; my flesh is mine and am the only one responsible for my flesh. Nobody said that when you desire to move up in life, all the mountains will disappear. Your desire to achieve greatness does not mean the mountains will disappear. Things won't be smooth; there is a personal responsibility for the unfolding of your dream i.e. the flesh must be disciplined.

14. In a church setting, the way to overcome fornication and adultery is not to tell all the women to tie their hair and not wear short skirts or lip stick. Inside the dress there is a body and we can see under the dress - that is the power of imagination, your mind travels faster than the speed of light and will break every barrier and imagine; it's better you see something than imagine.

What you have imagined is a result of your own personal thoughts; if you have disciplined yourself, you can look and not be moved. That is not a license for women wearing provocative clothes in church.

15. The point is if you don't deal with it internally you can't deal with it externally.

16. You cannot control a man by putting restrictions on him; you control a man by teaching him God's ways. So, your prayer should be, 'Help me with self-discipline; strengthen my will Lord.'

17. You have a dream bigger than your immediate needs. Your mind must be renewed with God's word and your body, i.e. your flesh must be disciplined to yield to the instructions from your spirit man to conform to God's word. You are

transformed, translated, changed and have gone through a spiritual metamorphosis, by the renewing of your mind with God's word. Your soul is made up of your mind, your will and your emotions.

18. REMEMBER: The mind is the battleground. That is what the devil plays on. You see something, you focus your eyes, thoughts and attention on it and if you play around on that thought it becomes an imagination and if you don't check that imagination or what you are thinking on, it becomes a stronghold.

2 Corinthians 10:4-6 says, "The weapons of our warfare are not carnal but they are mighty through God to the pulling down of strongholds; casting down imaginations and every high thing that exalts itself above the knowledge of God bringing every thought to the obedience of Christ."

That's why Paul exhorts us in Philippians 4:6-8 to think thoughts that are true, honest, just, pure, lovely, worthy of praise and of good report.

19. Your body is made up of your five senses: your eyes for seeing, your ears for hearing, your mouth for tasting, nose for smelling, hands for touching.

The Bible says in Galatians 5:16,
"Walk in the spirit that ye may not fulfil the desires of the flesh."

20. Every temptation comes three ways, in other words you

are tempted in three major areas: The lust of the flesh; the lust of the eyes and the pride of life.

1 John 2:16 says, "For all that is in the world, the lust of the flesh, the lust of the eyes and the pride of life is not of the father, but is of the world."

21. The flimsy excuse that some people give is that the spirit is willing but the flesh is weak but you can't give that as an excuse for yielding to sin because even though God understands, he does not approve.

What is Temptation?
It is a solicitation to evil or an enticement to evil or sin as in Proverbs 1:10.

The word 'tempted' in Genesis means to try, test or to prove and it is from the Hebrew word 'Nissah'. - Genesis 22:1; James 1:13

The devil tempts you, but God proves you during that temptation, watching your attitude to see how you react and respond with His word.

The devil tempts in the area of your flesh whilst God proves you to try your heart. - Jeremiah 17:9, 10

God will prove your heart in the situation in which you are being tempted of the devil.

30 Things You Need to Know In Times Of Temptation

1. The devil is the tempter. (Matthew 4:3)

2. God is not the tempter. (James 1:12-16)

3. The devil has no respect for the one whom he tempts; he's not a respecter of who he tempts. He will tempt everyone. Typical example was that, even though he knew Jesus was the Son of God, he did not make any exceptions; he had no respect for His position and went ahead and tempted Him anyway.

4. The devil tempts every man. (James 1:14)

5. The devil will tempt you at the point of and in the area of your weakness; remember, you were once under his domain so he knows your area of weakness before you got saved, and that is the area in which he will tempt you to try to derail your Christian experience and accuse you before your Heavenly Father to derail your destiny. (Matthew 4:2-3; Ephesians 2:1-3, 10; Revelation 12:10)

6. The devil tempts every man in three main areas - the lust of the flesh, the lust of the eyes and the pride of life. (1 John 2:16) CAUTION: Watch what you hear, what you see and what you say and the circles you move in [associations]. (Genesis 3:6) That's how Eve was deceived.

7. Your flesh is always at war with your spirit, battling for supremacy against your spirit man, which is the 'real you'. (Galatians 5:16, 17) Paul said in Romans 7:15-24, 'The things I want to do, I find myself not doing and the things I don't want to do are rather the things I find myself doing;...... O wretched man that I am.........' For example, the number of times you want to pray or fast, but can't is a sign the tempter is at work.

8. You need to remember that when you gave your life to Christ, it was only your spirit man that got saved or born again, not your soul or mind, will or emotion or your body made up of your 5 senses. Your mind has to be continually renewed with God's word through study and your flesh must be subdued daily, die daily, kept under control and disciplined daily before it goes out of control in having its way in your life which will be disastrous for your Christian faith. (John 3:5-6; Romans 8:9-16)

9. After you give your life to Christ, after having been controlled by your body made up of your five senses all your life (sense of smell, sight, feeling, touch and taste), it will take your walking by your sixth sense of faith to enable you overcome and live a victorious life in this world. (Romans 1:17; 10:17; Hebrews 11:6; 1 John 5:3-5)

10. When you are tempted, you are tempted of your own lust and enticed, baited by your own evil desire (lust, passions). (James 1:14)

11. REMEMBER: The devil cannot make you sin, yield to sin or do anything you don't want to do. His job is to tempt you and it's your job to submit to God's Word and resist him and the temptation, remaining steadfast in the faith to overcome without yielding to the enticement to sin. (Romans 6:14; Proverbs 1:10; Psalm 1:1; James 4:7; 1 Peter 5:8)

12. Don't give him (Satan) any place, territory, foothold or loophole in your life. (Ephesians 4:27)

13. Remember the devil is your adversary (enemy - he's not your friend, he hates your guts and fears the exercising of your faith); he walks about, roams around seeking whom he may devour but you have power over him to resist him steadfast in the faith. (Luke 10:19; 1 Peter 5:8-9)

14. Remember this: perfection, grounding, establishment, strengthening and settling will only come after every test, trial, suffering and overcoming of temptation. (1 Peter 5:10)

15. Don't mess with or play with the fire of temptation; it will burn you. Scripture says in Proverbs 6:27-28, 'Can a man take fire in his bosom, and his clothes not be burned? Can one go upon hot coals, and his feet not be burned?'

In other words, 'Who takes fire in his hands and his clothes won't be burnt and who walks on fire and it does not burn his feet?'

16. Scripture says, 'If you break the hedge (of God's Word) around you, the snake will bite you.' (Ecclesiastes 10:8; Matthew 4:4; Hebrews 4:12)

17. Hide God's word in your heart so you will not sin against Him. (Psalm 119:11)

18. Watch and pray lest you enter into temptation. (Matthew 26:41)

19. Be aware of the seducing and enticing descendants of Delilah and Jezebel who are still around to seduce you and destroy you. (Judges 16; 1 Kings 16; 18; 19 21; 2 Kings 9; 1 Timothy 4:1; Revelation 2:20);

20. Be aware, be conscious of and be vigilant against strange women, strange men and strange children. (Proverbs 2:15; 5:3,20; 6:23-26; 7:5; 20:16; 22:14; 23:27,33; 27:13; Psalm 144:11)

21. The area in which I am tempted may not necessarily be the area in which you will be tempted; you've got to find, discover and know the area of your weakness and saturate yourself with God's word and promises for victory in that area so that when Satan comes, you have a specific Rhema word to resist him with as Jesus did in Matthew 4:1-11.

22. When temptation comes, it will take both prayer and the word to overcome it, not, just prayer or binding and loosing alone. The word will create power and resistance to the

temptation. (Matthew 4; Genesis 39; 1 John 5:4-5)

23. Sometimes we get tired and then we stop praying, studying God's word, meditating, witnessing, fellowshipping and worshipping. Anytime we do that, we can be taken; we can get worn out and having done all to stand, we sit instead of stand. (Hebrews 10:25; Joshua 1:8-9; Matthew 26:41; Ephesians 6:13; Psalm 34:1-3)

24. When certain avoidable temptations are rampant in your walk with God, check your life, judge yourself so as not to be judged so the devil will not be able to accuse you before God. Watch where you go, check the company you keep, the things you watch on TV, the books you read because you could have become lukewarm or are backsliding. Also, be very selective about those you call, 'friends', the company you keep, the places you go, what you watch or read or say or focus your eyes, ears and affections on.

Remember scripture says,
'Evil communication (bad company) corrupts good manners.' (1 Corinthians 15:33; Psalm 1:1-3; Colossians 3:1-25; Revelation 3:14-end)

25. Remember, pretty, attractive, seductive, enticing, beautiful women or handsome, macho men are not temptation - they are not the tempters, Satan is.

26. Never use the vocabulary or be caught making a statement such as, 'They made me do it', 'The devil made me do it', 'I

couldn't help myself', 'Something clouded my face and my thinking', 'I don't know what happened', etc. Such statements reveal the level of your ignorance of God's word and who you are in Christ. ASK GOD FOR HELP AGAINST DEMONIC REMOTE CONTROLS; e.g. Zechariah 3. You can resist any temptation and you can do all things through Christ who strengthens you; God is a very present help in the time of need and is with you in trouble to deliver you and honour you. Find the way of escape and stop making excuses. (Philippians 4:13; Zechariah 4:6; Psalm 27:9; 46:1; 124:8; Psalm 91:14,15; 1 Corinthians 10:13)

27. Know that sin is common to all men (women alike) and is no new thing. (1 Corinthians 10:13; Galatians 5:13)

28. You can be a believer (Born again Christian and even a preacher) and still sin, lie, steal, fornicate, murder, gossip, backbite, be a conman, commit adultery, etc. What you need to do to avoid doing any of these and more is to renew your mind with God's Word, do what God's word says always remaining vigilant against sin/temptation and discipline your flesh always. (Romans 12:1-2)

29. Remember, sin will bring disgrace to you, bring you down to the pit and destroy your soul. (Proverbs 6:26, 32-33)

30. Remember the wages of sin is death. Sin separates you from God, makes you feel guilty, destroys you and kills you eventually. (Romans 6:23a)

30 Do's And Don'ts – Things To Do And Things Not To Do:

1. Find the area(s) of your weakness and find/search the scriptures for appropriate scriptures that deal with the temptation that often overtakes you or the weights and sins that easily besets you and let the word fortify and dominate you to the point of your developing a strong immovable resistance to that temptation. (Matthew 4:4; 2 Timothy 2:15; Hebrews 12:1-2)

2. Don't get pre-occupied in prayer with the temptation only; find the way of escape. (1 Corinthians 10:13)

3. Obey God. (Proverbs 4:20-24)

4. Know, be assured and be fully persuaded that God will not suffer you to be tempted, tried or tested above or beyond that which you are able to bear. (1 Corinthians 10:13)

5. Don't trust yourself to the point of depending so much on your spirituality or human ability to resist sin, because the arm of flesh will fail you. A preacher put it this way, 'You can tame the lion, but you can't tame Delilah, flee!'

Scripture says in 1 Corinthians 10:12, 'Let him that thinks he standeth, take heed, lest he fall.'

Don't believe too much in yourself or your abilities to the extent that you express surprise and shock when you fall and find yourself saying 'How could I have done this?' or 'I can't believe that I could have done this!' Why? Because, 1 Samuel 2:9 says, 'By the arm of flesh shall no man prevail.'

And Micah 7:8 says 'Rejoice not against me, O mine enemy: when I fall (not, if I fall, but when I fall,) I shall arise..........'

So, you can fall if you don't remain vigilant. Remember, the arm of flesh fails; you can't depend on it but you can depend on God's word, so, saturate yourself with it.

Scriptural proofs are:
1 Corinthians 6:18, 'Flee fornication.........'
2 Timothy 2:22, 'Flee also youthful lusts.......'
1 Corinthians 10:14, 'Flee from idolatry'
1 Timothy 6:11, '........Man of God, flee these things; and follow after righteousness..........'

6. Submit yourself to God first, then, resist the devil and he will flee from you. (James 4:7)

7. Don't condemn yourself when you are taken in a fault or miss the mark. Know that you have been saved by grace through faith. Try again and depend on the grace of God and His Word. (2 Corinthians 12:9)

8. When you fall, rise up and continue in the race. (Micah 7:8; Psalm 51 [David rose up]; 1 Corinthians 9:24; Philippians 3:13-14; Philemon vs. 1-22 [Onesimus])

9. Remember, you are not a failure until you quit.

10. Remember, it's not over until you win.

11. Don't deceive yourself into thinking that idolatry, adultery, fornication, murder, etc. are the only sins or temptations. No; anger and bad temper that leads to wrath is a sin, lying, gossiping, backbiting, strife, worry, rebellion to authority, disloyalty; destroying your pastor's ministry; anxiety, unbelief, deceit, unforgiveness, bitterness, etc. are all sins. (Matthew 5:44; Mark 11:25; Proverbs 6:16; Galatians 5:19-21)

12. Don't yield to the devil's tricks or enticements to sin through the use of falsely or inaccurately quoted scriptures. Know the Word for yourself. Let the Word dwell in you richly and study to show yourself approved unto God, rightly dividing the word of truth to know what God's word is and what it isn't. (Matthew 4:1-11; Genesis 3:1-7; Colossians 3:16; 2 Timothy 2:15)

13. Don't keep sinning and use 1 John 1:9 as a bail out. GROW! (1 Peter 2:2; Matthew 4:4; Psalm 1:1-3)

14. Hide God's Word in your heart that you won't sin deliberately against Him. (Psalm 119:11)

15. Let the word be in your mouth, your heart, before your eyes, study it, listen to it and hear it through your ears, say it and do it. (Joshua 1:8-9; Proverbs 4:20-22)

16. Don't let anyone's mistakes, faults of fall discourage you or keep you from continuing in the race; work out your own salvation with fear and trembling. – Philippians 2:12

17. Strive against sin and the lusts that war against your soul. Remember, you have not as yet resisted to the point of blood. (1 Peter 2:11; Hebrews 12:4)

18. Flee youthful lust. (2 Timothy 2:22; 1 Corinthians 6:18-20; 10:14; 1 Timothy 6:11)

19. Submit yourself to God (His Word), Resist the devil and he will flee from you. (James 4:7)

20. Always occupy, guard, protect, arm yourself with the word of God and put on the whole armour of God. (Matthew 4:1-11; Ephesians 6:1-18)

21. Neither give place to sin, temptation or the devil. (Ephesians 4:27)

22. Be sober and vigilant at all times. (1 Peter 5:8-9)

23. Let your heart be fixed and established, trusting in the Lord. (Psalm 112:7-8)

24. Don't be critical or judgmental of anyone because, when you do, you open yourself up or expose yourself to certain temptations. (Proverbs 6:16; Galatians 6:1-5)

25. Never say, 'God sent me this temptation to teach me a lesson or something in particular.' Cast that mentality out, for the Bible says in John 14:26 that, the Holy Spirit is your teacher, not temptation. God sent you His Holy Spirit as your teacher and my Teacher.

26. Lay aside every weight and the sin that easily besets or harasses you, looking unto Jesus the author and finisher or perfecter of your faith. (Hebrews 12:1-2)

27. If sin pays wages which is death as stated in Romans 6:23, then, not yielding to sin pays wages as well in the form of better wages and lasting or everlasting salary in the form of eternal life. Let me put it this way: IF WAGES ARE PAID FOR SINNING, THEN, SURELY, MORE OR BETTER WAGES ARE PAID FOR 'FAITHING' i.e. walking by faith - obeying and acting on God's word that you believe – walking, living and observing to do God's word (Joshua 1:8,9).

28. If you know yourself, you will win in times of temptation. Don't pretend you don't have a shortcoming or weakness; rather acknowledge it, find scriptures to deal with it and overcome it. (Psalm 119:11)

29. Sin shall not reign in your mortal body for you to obey it in the lusts thereof. (Romans 6:12)

30. Sin has no power or dominion over you, for the law of the spirit of life in Christ Jesus has made you free from the

law of sin and death. (Romans 6:14; Romans 8:2)

SCRIPTURES ON YOUR VICTORY OVER SIN:

Galatians 3:13-14, "Christ hath redeemed us from the curse of the law, being made a curse for us: for it is written, Cursed is every one that hangeth on a tree: That the blessing of Abraham might come on the Gentiles through Jesus Christ; that we might receive the promise of the Spirit through faith."

THANK GOD: Christ has redeemed us from the curse of the law being made a curse for us.

ADDITIONAL RECOMMENDED READING:
Romans 6:1-23;7; 8:1-39; 1st, 2nd and 3rd Epistles of John; Revelation 3

LASTLY, AVOID UNFORGIVENESS AT ALL COST!!!! "An eye for an eye can only lead to blindness." - MARGARET ATWOOD

KEY SCRIPTURES:
Jeremiah 8:22, 'Is there no balm in Gilead; is there no physician there? why then is not the health of the daughter of my people recovered?'

James 5:16, 'Confess your faults one to another, and pray one for another, that ye may be healed. The effectual fervent prayer of a righteous man availeth much.'

FACTS ABOUT FORGIVENESS AND UNFORGIVENESS

1. FORGIVENESS IS A HEALING BALM - When you forgive your neighbour, you lift burdens off your shoulder.

2. Unforgiveness brings and keeps sicknesses and diseases on and in your body.

3. Unforgiveness ages - Joy and laughter increases your life-span; unforgiveness reduces your life-span.

4. Unforgiveness is not a sin you commit but a sin you refuse to let go of.

5. Unforgiveness is a deadly poison i.e. venom.

6. Unforgiveness is murder in its embryo form - it can lead to murder.

7. Unforgiveness makes your offerings hypocritical, pretentious and unacceptable.

8. There is a physical and emotional prize we pay when we grow bitter and resentful and operate in an unforgiving spirit.

9. If you refuse to forgive, your sins are retained or remain in you.

10. Unforgiveness hinders answers to your prayers and faith.

11. AVOID UNFORGIVENESS AT ALL COST!!

12. FORGIVENESS IS FOR YOUR BENEFIT!

13. FORGIVENESS IS IN YOUR INTEREST!

14. FORGIVENESS IS A HEALING BALM!

15. FORGIVENESS IS IN YOUR BEST INTEREST!!

[Order a copy of MY BOOK: DESTINY-BLOCKERS AND DESTINY-MAKERS from www.houseofjudah.org. uk]

SECTION TWO

MAKING THE RIGHT CHOICE OF A MARRIAGE PARTNER

Chapter
Seven

WHAT IS MARRIAGE?

WHERE PURPOSE IS UNKNOWN, ABUSE IS INEVITABLE!!!

Proverbs 4:7, 'Wisdom is the principal thing; therefore get wisdom: and with all thy getting get understanding.'

Proverbs 21:1, 'The king's heart is in the hand of the LORD, as the rivers of water: he turneth it whithersoever he will.'

Proverbs 21:16, 'The man that wandereth out of the way of understanding shall remain in the congregation of the dead.'

DON'T ENTER ANYTHING YOU ARE NOT SURE ABOUT!

At the root of everything outstanding including relationships, is understanding.

SO, IN ALL YOUR GETTING, GET UNDERSTANDING!

ON MARRIAGE AND RELATIONSHIPS

- Marriage is a good thing.
- Marriage is like a precious gem.
- Marriage is God's idea.
- Marriage is still a good idea because it is GOD's idea.
- A healthy "house" is the key to both a healthy church and a healthy society.
- Marriage is a lifetime commitment.
- Marriage means that everything is shared.
- Marriage involves being with the same person for long periods of time.
- Marriage is something like a big amplifier.
- Marriage is honourable – Hebrews 13:4.
- Marriage is an institution.
- You enter an institution not to change it, but to abide by its rules so you can benefit from all that it has to offer you, to make you a better person, more effective and prominent, a master at what you do, to graduate with distinction, increase your salary scale, go into the world and make a great impact in life from what you discovered and applied and eventually recommend it to others.

- Success in marriage does not depend on spouses committing themselves to **EACH OTHER** as much as it does to their committing themselves to **MARRIAGE**, the unchanging institution that they have **MUTUALLY** entered into. Your commitment as long as you remain in that institution is to the institution and so is the marriage [institution]. So, no matter what happens, you are committed to what you committed your life to – the institution of marriage.

- It's not who you love but what you love – honour and esteem marriage itself.

- Marriage is a steady unchanging perfect institution entered into by two imperfect people who are constantly changing as they grow and mature. Whenever you are entering marriage, commit yourself to the marriage, not the person, because people – everybody grows and change takes place. If you commit yourself to whoever you marry and think they will remain the same physically, you will be disappointed.

- Marriage is two imperfect people committing themselves to a perfect institution, by making perfect vows from imperfect lips.

- A Happy Marriage is No Accident - you work at it by understanding and engaging what we have captioned THE LOVE COMBINATION ANOINTING **[COMBO]**.

Next, we will look at this LOVE COMBINATION ANOINTING [COMBO] explaining the different kinds of love that makes your marriage blissful and a blessing to others. [***For additional insight on what marriage is, order our newest books: 101 TIPS FOR A GREAT MARRIAGE and WHAT HUSBANDS WANT AND WHAT WIVES 'REALLY' WANT from our website: www.houseofjudah.org.uk]

- Marriage is bigger than the two people in it.

Remember: LOVE IS NOT JUST A FEELING, BUT A DISCIPLINE. IT IS A CHOICE.

- It takes only a few minutes to get married, but building a marriage requires a lifetime.

- **Understanding LOVE:** The New Testament was translated from the Greek to English and from that Greek word, 'LOVE' comes four different meanings as follows: Bible writers used four different Greek words for Love:

1. **Eros** - sexual love; from which you get the word erotic; erotic book shop, erotica; love in order to get something from you; this is physical love; married love; mutual desire between a man and a woman. This is love that is blessed of God and is found in Song of Solomon.

2. **Storge** (Pronounced storg'ay) – family love. Romans 12:10 says we are to treat Christians like we treat members of our own families – with respect.

3. **Phileo** (pronounced fil-eh' o) – the love of friendship, the affection we feel for people in friendly relationships. Phileo is a word that has to do with feelings; feelings for people; is a word for friendship love; warm affectionate love of friends; how to be affectionate. Love because of friendship; Phileo also has an element of giving and receiving, an exchange, directly or indirectly.

4. **Agape** – (pronounced ag-ah' pay) divine love; love in spite of; unconditional love; agape is the kind of love that just gives and gives and gives never really asking

for anything in return. That is God's divine kind of love for us which we must have for humanity.

- **Agape,** however is unselfish. It is the totally unselfish love of God toward His people; it gives and gives and keeps on giving never really asking for anything in exchange. It is a beautiful concept of love not based on emotions or feelings; it is actually a love by choice, a love that doesn't look for affinity and gives us the ability to love even that which is unlovely, or the unlovable; it always has the best interest of the other person. GOD DOESN'T CHANCE TO LOVE US, HE CHOOSES TO LOVE US and so do we as Born-Again Christians. LOVE IS A CHOICE; IT IS A DISCIPLINE, WE CHOOSE TO LOVE IN SPITE OF.

In summary:
Agape is the divine love, has the best interest of the other
Phileo is the love of friendship or brotherly love,
Storge is the love of family, and
Eros is the love of man for woman

QUESTION: What kind of Love do I need in my marriage?

ANSWER: The Kind Of Love Everyone Needs In Order To Have a Successful, Happy, Fruitful, Secure, Sustaining, & Satisfying Marriage & Family Life Is - What I Call: Or THE LOVE COMBINATION ANOINTING [COMBO]

What I mean by Love Combination Anointing is, all the four kinds of love integrated to work together, hand in hand for fulfilment. This is not an either/or proposition by asking what is your preference or choice such as do you want to choose an affectionate love for people and friends or emotional love based on considerations and the act of the will or loving in spite of. There isn't just a single choice to be made. All of the four kinds of love are involved, are crucial and an absolute necessity. Let's look at the various combinations and how they work as we deliberately put them together and work them.

SUMMARY

Agape and eros in a marriage makes it a Christian marriage – an unselfish, thoughtful, loving, considerate marriage union.

Agape and storge in a family makes it a Christian family – a family that is not a civil war or a contest or a volcano ready to erupt or explode, but a family that is solid and strong, a house built on the firm foundation of God's love and His word.

Agape and phileo in a friendship makes it a friendship that is based not on external considerations. It is a friendship that will weather the storms, the adversities, and the setbacks in life – a friendship that will survive no matter how strong the wind is blowing or the earthquakes, or hurricanes of life.

Agape is available in all the relationships of life because Romans 5:5 says it is shed abroad in our hearts by the Holy Ghost.

PRAYER: Pray this prayer of dedication:

'Lord, I'm a candidate for **agape**. *What I need and my marriage relationship, friendship relationships and family relationships need is more*

of Your **agape** *love, so I can improve and excel in every relationship I have.* **Agape** *will place an unselfish, sacrificial element in my marriage. It will strengthen my family and put solidarity in my friendships to keep them from being exploitative and manipulative. I pray, Lord, that You will work to develop Your* **agape** *love in me, to make me what you want me to be, so that Your love shows through every area of my life for all to see and benefit from. I thank you for answered prayer in Jesus' Name. Amen.'*

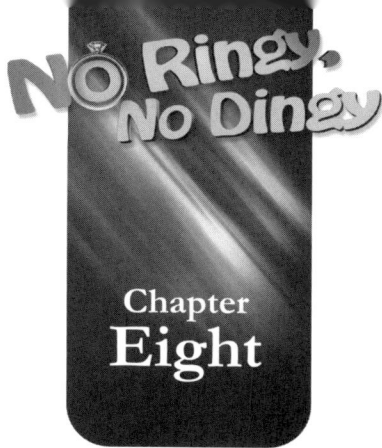

101 REASONS WHY PEOPLE GET MARRIED

101 QUALITIES THAT VARIOUS PEOPLE LOOK FOR IN A PROSPECTIVE MARRIAGE PARTNER

IT IS BETTER TO BUILD A FENCE ON TOP OF A CLIFF THAN A HOSPITAL AT THE BOTTOM OF THE CLIFF! [Order my book: **'50 Common Mistakes Singles Make'** to help you make the right decisions based on prioritising destiny and adequate relevant information.]

He who chooses the beginning of a road also chooses its outcome. So watch what road you choose and why!

Some of the Most Important Qualities People Look For, In A Marriage Partner are as follows:

Various Opinions:

1. Someone to help me pay my bills.
2. Good communicator.
3. Funny [has a sense of humour].
4. Good lover and good cook.
5. One who is not a career person.
6. One I can go to parties with.
7. One who will give me everything I want.
8. No negative or destructive addictions.
9. A woman who will give me many children.
10. Well dressed with good taste, classic.
11. Respectful.
12. Affectionate.
13. Someone who will spoil me.
14. Helpful.
15. Energetic.
16. Strong and confident.
17. Emotionally secure.
18. Good-looking.
19. Tall, dark and handsome.
20. Pretty / beautiful.
21. A visionary.
22. Can write without mistakes in French, Spanish and English.
23. Financially stable [Financial stability].
24. Smart/astute.
25. Strong and stable emotionally and physically.
26. Matured.
27. Not lazy but hard working.
28. Good conflict management skills.

29. Good people skills.
30. Ambitious.
31. Faithful.
32. Dependable.
33. Punctual.
34. Responsible.
35. Engages his mental faculties well to create wealth and make sound productive decisions.
36. Things in common.
37. Passion.
38. Someone whose parents are rich.
39. Religious.
40. Goals-oriented.
41. Honest.
42. Physical attraction/compatibility.
43. The capacity for true intimacy.
44. Hastiness or fear of growing old or your contemporaries leaving you behind.
45. Immigration status/Citizenship.
46. Loyalty and commitment.
47. Works hard to bring money home.
48. Friendship.
49. A foreign national to take me abroad.
50. Patient and understanding.
51. Acceptance.
52. Cordiality and agreement over money. (Amos 3:3)
53. Not difficult to live with.
54. Not Stubborn.
55. Fidelity [Abstinence from Infidelity].
56. Agreements over children's training and development.

57. Not prone to physical or mental abuse.
58. Not distractive or a distracter.
59. Unconditional love, stability and consistency.
60. Generous [Great provider].
61. Confident and courageous.
62. Warmth.
63. Rich.
64. Millionaire.
65. Sweep me off my feet.
66. Caring.
67. Supportive.
68. No annoying habits or just a few.
69. Not grumpy and stingy.
70. Has the potential for loving, having and maintaining children.
71. Exhibits and demonstrates the **essential ingredients of Love** (The Five Love Languages: Words of Affirmation; Quality Time; Gifts; Acts of Service; Physical Touch).
72. A man who will meet my emotional needs.
73. A woman who will meet my sexual needs.
74. Loving and affectionate.
75. A home to be proud of and a sense of security.
76. A person who will help me to make the marriage work and give his or her all for the betterment of the marriage.
77. A person who is stable and kind.
78. A person who is slow to anger, wrath and to speaking guile.
79. A person who is a good worker and who has a good job.
80. Someone who understands the art of compromise.

81. Someone who values honesty, respect and loyalty in self and others.
82. Someone who ISN'T high maintenance, but can just enjoy hanging out.
83. Someone who can go with the flow and not freak out when things are going wrong.
84. Someone who can still love my friends and family because they're a part of me even if they do manage to drive me crazy from time to time.
85. Someone who likes kids, but isn't afraid to be authoritative when he needs to be.
86. Someone who is gentle with animals and old people and babies.
87. Someone who's prepared to be locked in with a single person for life.
88. Someone willing to give up a great deal of freedom to be

with me.
89. Someone willing to consult on most issues if not all.
90. Someone willing to have to work to maintain and build their human qualities.
91. A person who will be a good mother or father.
92. Someone who's always there for me and to take care of me.
93. Someone who will help us get more for our efforts.
94. Someone who is decisive.
95. Someone devoted to me alone.
96. Someone with a generational mindset and global world view.
97. Sexually attractive: Sexual attraction is one of the basic

reasons why people get married. Sometimes this sexual attraction, which is a natural response to a basic emotional need, can develop into love. In some cases, this love may have some permanence; in others it may be no more than a fleeting passion – a passion that is satisfied in sexual intercourse and does not look for anything deeper.

98. Procreation: A desire for and responsible with children: All couples expect to have children as the fruit of their relationship. Having children of their own does not only satisfy the social expectations of the couple but it is also basic to all living creatures that they should reproduce; it satisfies an instinctive urge in the couple.

99. Assurance and security: To assure themselves of a guaranteed future and security: People get married to have regular and dependable sources of income, a house to live in, a regular supply of food, clothes to wear, and maybe wealth to display with dual parents to raise their children.

100. For companionship: Perhaps the most important reason why people get married is that they look for someone with whom they can share life together as a unit in mutual relationship; in their marriage, they chart their own course and their own unique lifestyle. What enriches this relationship is the couple's ability to compromise and change some aspects of their personal lifestyles so that each can accommodate the other partner. To attain this is no mean task. It requires gentle but firm effort and willingness to succeed in spite of all odds.

101. Differences: I want someone uniquely different from myself. Some get married because male and female are different: We have to take time to understand the people we have chosen as our life-long partners. We often clash just because male and female are different – yet we fail to recognize that these differences between men and women are one of the reasons why men and women want each other! Through these differences we complement each other – that is, each contributes to the marriage something that the other does not possess.

God has given to women great abilities to endure pain, exposure, shock, and illness. INTUITIVE: they sense things and dangers and upcoming temptation and seducers that the men can't see.

Women are more intuitive than men. As a result women sense things which men, with their reliance upon logic, are prone to overlook. How many men fail to appreciate this special gift which God has given to women! Perhaps if men understand women and pay more attention to their advice they can avoid many things that bring unhappiness, strife, arguments and disagreements into their homes.

Women regard things on the personal level much more than men. In any situation women think first how the outcome of their actions affects their homes and their relationships with their partners and children. From the foregoing it can be seen that women and men approach things from entirely dissimilar points of reference. Women rely on intuition whereas men on logic and are prone to overlook some of the things that women simply "sense".

Men need to understand that to the woman her home is an extension of her personality. That is why she is so much concerned about the fabric, chairs, the curtains, kind of food, cooking utensil, home décor and everything that goes to make a place worth living in. On the contrary, the man may be concerned about his work and how to bring enough money home for the upkeep of the family. The demands of the wife will therefore sometimes seem unimportant to the man: but they make all the difference to the woman. For instance when a newborn baby arrives in their home, the man [father] just looks at the baby and is satisfied; however the woman [mother] is not that satisfied with just looking; she will examine the fingers, toes, limbs, joints, hair, eyes, nose, ear, etc. to satisfy herself that everything is intact. – Why? Women are detailed.

[For what men want and what women really want get my books: WHAT HUSBANDS WANT AND WHAT WIVES 'REALLY' WANT and 101 TIPS FOR A GREAT MARRIAGE from our website: www.houseofjudah.org.uk]

MEN ARE LOGICAL BEINGS WHILST WOMEN ARE EMOTIONAL BEINGS! THIS IS A COMPLIMENT [A PLUS] NOT A CRITICISM [A NEGATIVE]! On the contrary the man needs financial security to make him happy, and will be more concerned about how to make ends meet whilst the woman's pride is in her man satisfying her and being there for her. In sexual matters men have a TRIANGULAR DRIVE UNLIKE WOMEN WHO HAVE A TRAPEZIUM DRIVE: Men act like an electric light – they quickly get into action, and demand satisfaction. On the contrary, women take a long time to warm up – they are like the electric iron, which is not ready for use until sometime after it has been switched on.

These psychological differences in men and women need not work against each other. Indeed the couple should work hand in hand for the enrichment of the marriage.

Neither men nor women are wrong in their approach to issues, situations and problems. Their different responses arise just because they are psychologically different. These differences, if accepted and constructively used, can be assets to the marriage relationship, and not liabilities.

REMEMBER: Very often what you should seek depends entirely upon who and what you are, what you consider important, your idea of deal-breakers, your values and beliefs but ultimately it must be about and for destiny fulfilment.

What women don't want:
- Inept come-on lines [fake raps]
- Sloppy looks
- Self-centeredness
- Arrogance
- Slimy, over eagerness

- Roughness
- A 'weakling' who faints at the slightest sign of challenge
- Competition
- Dishonesty
- Infidelity
- An Aimless man
- A Lazy man
- An abuser
- Molester
- Indecisiveness
- Unfaithfulness
- A non-provider
- Hurtful words that cut deep
- Flattery
- Making them look stupid
- Annoying habits
- Sex without adequate preparation
- Always consulting with parents before making crucial decisions
- Makes decisions unilaterally without her involvement

What men don't want:
Rejection
Anger
Complaints
Criticism
Coldness
Moodiness
Degradation

Timetable on sex
Competition
Dishonesty
Infidelity
Rudeness
Control
Manipulation

WHAT BOTH MALE AND FEMALES WANT: 1 Corinthians 13

Love that Suffers long, and is kind; does not envy, not vaunt itself, is not puffed up, does not behave itself unseemly, seeks not her own, is not easily provoked, thinks no evil; does not rejoice in iniquity, but rejoices in the truth; bears all things, believes all things, hopes all things, endures all things and does not fail [never fails].

WHAT EVERY ONE SHOULD KNOW ABOUT DIVORCE BEFORE THEY GET MARRIED

ON THE ISSUE OF MARRIAGE, DIVORCE AND REMARRIAGE:

20 Commands Concerning Marriage and Remarriage:
- 1 Corinthians 7

1. Let every man have his own wife (vs. 2).

2. Let every woman have her own husband (vs. 2).

3. Let the husband meet the sexual needs of his own wife (vs. 3-4).

4. Let the wife meet the sexual needs of her own husband (vs. 3-4).

5. Defraud not each other in sexual matters - pay your conjugal vows (vs. 5).

6. Come together again after you have consented to live continent for a period of time for reasons pertaining to fasting and prayer (vs. 5).

7. Let both men and women marry if they have battles of self-control (vs. 9).

8. Let not the wife depart from her husband (vs.10).

9. If she does depart, let her remain unmarried or reconciled to her husband (vs. 11).

10. Let not the husband divorce his wife (vs.11).

11. Let not the Christian man divorce the non-Christian wife if she be pleased to dwell with him: reasons (vs. 12-16).

12. Let not the Christian wife divorce her non-Christian husband if he be pleased to dwell with her (vs.13-16).

13. If the unbeliever departs and refuses to live with the Christian, let him depart. Do not force continuance of the marriage. The Christian is freed from the marriage bonds IN SUCH CASES (vs. 15).

14. Let every man or woman remain as he or she was when each became a Christian (vs. 17-24). That is, do not use Christianity as an excuse to break up your home and perhaps another, seeking a new companion.

15. If you are bound/married to a wife, seek not to be loosed or separated or divorced from her (vs. 27). That is, do not get a divorce, regardless of the past. Stay in the same calling and state in which you were saved. (vs. 17-24) [EXEMPTION CLAUSE: refer to point 21 below]

16. **Special cases related to Newly converted Christians (Use with care).** If you are loosed/separated or divorced from a wife, seek not another wife (vs. 27). If you do marry, however, you have not sinned (vs. 28).

17. You that have wives, live as though you did not have them (vs. 29-31); i.e. live free from anxiety (vs. 32-35).

18. Let the father who has a daughter of marriageable age be free to give her in marriage. It is no sin for him to do so for the virgin to marry (vs. 36-38).

19. The wife is bound by law to be/remain married as long as the husband lives/is still alive (vs. 39). Marriage is for the lifetime of the husband or wife. AMEN.

20. Christians must remarry only fellow Christians when partners die (vs. 39), i.e. if they want to remarry.

21. DON'T TOLERATE PHYSICAL OR SEXUAL ABUSE IN YOUR MARRIAGE – GET HELP AND COUNSELLING BEFORE YOU ARE KILLED AND DISMEMBERED!!

YOUR BODY IS THE TEMPLE OF THE HOLY GHOST!!!

DIVORCE AS SHOWN IN THE BIBLE

DIVORCE, as a word, occurred only once throughout the whole Bible in Jeremiah 3:8. Therefore, it is an unpopular word in the Bible. LESSON: Don't get involved in it. LOOK BEFORE YOU LEAP!

DIVORCED, as a word occurred four times in the entire Bible in the following passages:
Leviticus 21:14; 22:13
Numbers 30:9
Matthew 5:32

DIVORCEMENT, occurred six times in the entire Bible as found in:
Deuteronomy 24:1; 24:3
Isaiah 50:1
Matthew 5:31; 19:7
Mark 10:4

CONCLUSION:

Marriage is honourable in all things, and the bed undefiled: but whoremongers and adulterers God will judge. (Hebrews 13:4)

Marriage is a BLESSED and PERFECT institution and a thing practised on this earth only. (Matthew 22:30; Mark 12:25; Luke 20:34-35)

But everyone is invited to the marriage supper of the LAMB, which is the only everlasting marriage. GET READY FOR THIS MARRIAGE SUPPER OF THE LAMB BY BEING BORN AGAIN. (John 3:3-5)

BLESSED ARE THEY WHICH ARE CALLED UNTO THE MARRIAGE SUPPER OF THE LAMB…….. These are the true sayings of GOD. (Revelation 19:9)

THE SPIRIT AND THE BRIDE SAY, COME. LET HIM THAT HEARETH SAY, COME. LET HIM THAT IS AN ATHEIST COME. LET HIM TAKE THE WATER OF LIFE FREELY. (Revelation 22:17)

Blessed are those who hear and observe to do as commanded….

Chapter

Ten

MAKING THE RIGHT CHOICE OF A MARRIAGE PARTNER

Psalm 32:8-9, 'I will instruct thee and teach thee in the way which thou shalt go: I will guide thee with mine eye. Be ye not as the horse, or as the mule, which have no understanding: whose mouth must be held in with bit and bridle, lest they come near unto thee.'

The main purpose of God for your life is not getting married first. IT IS TO FULFIL DESTINY! YOUR MARRIAGE PARTNER IS TO HELP YOU FULFIL THAT DESTINY, NOT THE OTHER WAY ROUND! The whole duty of man is to fear God and obey His commands and fulfill his vision (Ecclesiastes 12:13; 1 John 3:8; Jeremiah 29:11; Proverbs 29:18; 22:29; 27:8)

Genesis 2:18, 'And the LORD God said, It is not good that the man should be alone; I will make him an help meet for him.'

It is not good that a man be alone……

Psalm 68:6a, 'God setteth the solitary in families: he bringeth out those which are bound with chains: …'

It is God's plan, desire and responsibility to bring the lone person into the security of a family unit because GOD IS PRO-FAMILY and builds revelationally, [By revelation, i.e. the Word] relationally [Through family relations] and generationally [with generations in mind].

GOD IS NOT INTERESTED IN SEEING PEOPLE SUFFERING FROM LONELINESS.

In Genesis 2:18, God initiated the process of solving Adam's aloneness. God observed the need to get Adam in the family. It is said that people's loneliness become acute when they attend weddings. Nevertheless, don't be hasty in your decision-making about marriage out of fear because fear brings torment but perfect [mature] love casts out fear. Have faith in God (Mark 11:23) to empower you to make the right decisions.

If you don't exercise your faith, you will make the wrong decisions. Blaming yourself for not getting married to that man or woman who came along earlier to propose to you ten or fifteen years ago is not helpful to your destiny. DON'T LIVE IN THE PAST! WHEN PEOPLE MOVE ON, MOVE ON WITH SPEED SWIFTLY!!

When you are bound by the past and in the past you cannot move into the future. Take responsibility for where you are now and believe God today for a better tomorrow. (Jeremiah 29:11; Psalm 30:5)

"Control your destiny or someone else will." - Jack Welch, CEO General Electric Company

He who controls the past controls the future. – George Orwell, 1984

[On how to control your past, refer to chapter three]

NO RINGY, NO DINGY

Songs of Solomon 1:16-17, 'Behold, thou art fair, my beloved, yea, pleasant: also our bed is green. The beams of our house are cedar, and our rafters of fir.'

OUR BED IS GREEN [VIRGINITY]!

In the kingdom or in church, going to bed with somebody should not be the beginning of any relationship. Every relationship must begin with brother-sister relationship based first of all on friendship PHILEO. [Refer to chapter seven]

The excuse some give for initiating the relationship with romance or sex is so as to test things if they will function before you buy them. YOU ARE NOT AN APPARATUS FOR EXPERIMENT. YOUR PRICE IS

FAR ABOVE RUBIES!!!

That is the risk they must take – DELAYED GRATIFICATION!

This test is not applicable to a marriage relationship. You don't test the man or woman sexually; rather, you test each other's character, loyalty, faithfulness and to see if it's God's will as to whether you are meant for each other, compatible for each other's destiny/purpose, if you suit each other and can live together eventually as husband and wife till death do you part with destiny as the focus.

Christians are different from the world, so we cannot do what the world does. (Matthew 5:13-14)

1. WE ARE IN THIS WORLD BUT NOT OF THIS WORLD.

2. WE ARE THE LIGHT OF THE WORLD, GIVING ILLUMINATION AND ENLIGHTENMENT IN THE MIDST OF DARKNESS.

3. WE ARE A CITY SET ON A HILL THAT PEOPLE LOOK UP TO FOR DIRECTION.

4. AND WE ARE THE SALT OF THE EARTH PLACED HERE FOR THE ULTIMATE PRESERVATION OF LIFE AND TO BRING TASTE TO THIS TASTELESS WORLD.

So, we are not the same and so the principles we live by are totally different.

The basis of our decisions is totally different. The heathen see things from the world's perspective; we see things from God's perspective. God's view of and on everything is what we desire to get ourselves involved in.

King Solomon is describing his intended spouse here:

YOU ARE FAIR AND BEAUTIFUL: Song 4:1, 'Behold, thou art fair, my love; behold, thou art fair; thou hast doves' eyes within thy locks: thy hair is as a flock of goats, that appear from mount Gilead.'

YOUR TEETH ARE WHITE/CRISPY CLEAN AND ATTRACTIVE: vs. 2, 'Thy teeth are like a flock of sheep that are even shorn, which came up from the washing; whereof every one bear twins, and none is barren among them.'

YOU SPEECH IS COMELY, SMOOTH, DECENT, NOT ROUGH or RUDE: vs. 3, 'Thy lips are like a thread of scarlet, and thy speech is comely: thy temples are like a piece of a pomegranate within thy locks.'

YOUR NECK IS LIKE A TOWER: I CAN FIND SAFETY LYING THERE: vs. 4, 'Thy neck is like the tower of David builded for an armoury, whereon there hang a thousand bucklers, all shields of mighty men.'

YOUR BREASTS ARE YOUNG: YOU ARE IN YOUR PRIME: vs. 5-6, 'Thy two breasts are like two young roes that are twins, which feed among the lilies. Until the day break, and the shadows flee away, I will get me to the mountain of myrrh, and to the hill of frankincense.'

YOU ARE FAIR AND THERE IS NO SPOT OR BLEMISH IN YOU: vs. 7-8, 'Thou art all fair, my love; there is no spot in thee. Come with me from Lebanon, my spouse, with me from Lebanon: look from the top of Amana, from the top of Shenir and Hermon, from the lions' dens, from the mountains of the leopards.'

YOU HAVE RAVISHED MY HEART WITH YOUR LOOKS/EYES: vs. 9, 'Thou hast ravished my heart, my sister, my spouse; thou hast ravished my heart with one of thine eyes, with one chain of thy neck.'

YOU SMELL GOOD LIKE OINTMENTS AND SPICES: vs. 10, 'How fair is thy love, my sister, my spouse! how much better is thy love than wine! and the smell of thine ointments than all spices!'

YOUR LIPS DROP LIKE HONEYCOMB AND YOUR GARMENTS SMELL GOOD: vs. 11, 'Thy lips, O my spouse, drop as the honeycomb: honey and milk are under thy tongue; and the smell of thy garments is like the smell of Lebanon.'

A GARDEN ENCLOSED, SHUT UP AND SEALED IS MY SISTER; NOT VIOLATED: vs. 12, 'A garden enclosed is my sister, my spouse; a spring shut up, a fountain sealed.'

YOUR PLANTS ARE AN ORCHARD OF VARIOUS FLAVOURS AND SPICES: vs. 13-15, 'Thy plants are an orchard of pomegranates, with pleasant fruits; camphire, with spikenard, Spikenard and saffron; calamus and cinnamon, with all trees of frankincense; myrrh and aloes, with all the chief spices: A fountain of gardens, a well of living waters, and streams from Lebanon.'

NO RINGY, NO DINGY!!!! YOU ONLY AWAKEN THE NORTH WIND FOR YOUR BELOVED TO COME INTO HIS GARDEN AND EAT HIS PLEASANT FRUITS AT THE END, WHEN EVERYTHING IS CULMINATED: vs. 16, 'Awake, O north wind; and come, thou south; blow upon my garden, that the spices thereof may flow out. Let my beloved come into his garden, and eat his pleasant fruits.'

Songs of Solomon 4:9-10, 'Thou hast ravished my heart, my sister, my spouse; thou hast ravished my heart with one of thine eyes, with one chain of thy neck. How fair is thy love, my sister, my spouse! how much better is thy love than wine! and the smell of thine ointments than all spices!'

In this passage of scripture, their relationship began as a brother and sister relationship – friendship [PHILEO].

REMEMBER: ROMANCE CLOUDS [DISTURBS] FOCUS!

Romance clouds your mind from seeing reality so you overlook the real and focus on what you want to see. You blank out what you should take note of.

Honest married couples will inform you that what keeps a marriage in hard or challenging times is the friendship that was built or developed early in life [before or during the courtship] where all or almost everything about each other's strengths and weaknesses were open for both parties to observe, scrutinise, examine, learn from and find rooms for compromise and decide whether to go ahead or not.

In Verse 9-10, he makes the following observations:

i. **She smells nice and in 1:16-17**

ii. **Songs 4:12 - she is sealed/enclosed [GREEN/ VIRGINITY]. HER GARDEN IS ENCLOSED; SHE IS CLOSED, NOT TOUCHED, INVADED, VIOLATED OR DISTURBED.**

Her response is found in verse 16. That is where she gives permission after marriage for sex, i.e. love-making. SEX IS PROOF OF LOVE IN MARRIAGE NOT LOVE IS PROOF OF SEX.

You prove your love for your spouse in the context of marriage with the sexual act, not before marriage.

RESPONSE: Chapter 5:1, 'I am come into **my garden, my sister, my spouse:** I have gathered my myrrh with my spice; I have eaten my honeycomb with my honey; I have drunk my wine with my milk: eat, O friends; drink, yea, drink abundantly, O beloved.'

<u>my</u> garden, <u>my</u> sister, <u>my</u> spouse: note the word '<u>my</u>'

WARNING:

Songs 2:7, 'I charge you, O ye daughters of Jerusalem, by the roes, and by the hinds of the field, that ye stir not up, nor awake my love, till he please.'

NO RINGY, NO DINGY!!!!! Don't awaken love or romantic feelings until you are ready in the context of marriage.

YOUTH DON'T PROPOSE; THEY BUILD FRIENDSHIPS, HAVE FRIENDS AND MAINTAIN FRIENDSHIP UNTIL……..

ADVICE FOR YOUTH: Don't propose or accept proposals; develop friendship first.

Don't awaken certain desires before their time.

Songs of Solomon, 4:4-5, 'Thy neck is like the tower of David builded for an armoury, whereon there hang a thousand bucklers, all shields of mighty men. Thy two breasts are like two young roes that are twins, which feed among the lilies.'

The roe is a very beautiful, graceful animal but can never be tamed. Its beauty has an aspect of it that is difficult to control. If you come across a roe and you excite it to run when it's not ready, it can be dangerous and deadly. So it is with certain passions. **UNTIL YOU ARE READY, LET LOVE SLEEP! UNTIL YOU ARE FULLY AND LEGALLY READY, LET CERTAIN PASSIONS REST! UNTIL YOU ARE READY, LET LOVE SLEEP AND FRIENDSHIP AWAKEN!!**

As the saying goes: LET SLEEPING DOGS LIE!

Songs 2:7, 'I charge you, O ye daughters of Jerusalem, by the roes, and by the hinds of the field, that ye stir not up, nor awake my love, till he please.'

Songs 3:5, 'I charge you, O ye daughters of Jerusalem, by the roes, and by the hinds of the field, that ye stir not up, nor awake my love, till he please.'

When you get too close to a person before marriage AND EVEN IN / AFTER MARRIAGE, [if not disciplined] a time comes when you desire to show, express and confirm your love and affection for them with the sexual act because that is the outward expression of such affections.

DON'T BELIEVE YOURSELF TOO MUCH…. LET HIM THAT THINK HE STANDETH TAKE HEED LEST HE FALL…..Hence King Solomon's advice in Songs 8:4, 'I charge you, O daughters of Jerusalem, that ye stir not up, nor awake my love, until he please.'

REMEMBER SOLOMON had seven hundred wives and three hundred girl friends so he has something to teach us on this subject!!!

1 Kings 11:3, 'And he had seven hundred wives, princesses, and three hundred concubines: and his wives turned away his heart.'

REMEMBER LOVE CANNOT BE QUENCHED: IT IS AS STRONG AS DEATH: Song 8:6-7, 'Set me as a seal upon thine heart, as a seal upon thine arm: for love is strong as death; jealousy is cruel as the grave: the coals thereof are coals of fire, which hath a most vehement flame. Many waters cannot quench love, neither can the floods drown it: if a man would give all the substance of his house for love, it would utterly be contemned.'

DOUBLE EMPHASIS: The same scripture found in Songs 2:7 is the same found in Songs 3:5:

Song 2:7, 'I charge you, O ye daughters of Jerusalem, by the roes, and by the hinds of the field, that ye stir not up, nor awake my love, till he please.'

Song 3:5, 'I charge you, O ye daughters of Jerusalem, by the roes, and by the hinds of the field, that ye stir not up, nor awake my love, till he please.'

DON'T STIR UP MY LOVE UNTIL YOU CAN PLEASE ME FULLY, SATISFACTORILY AND LEGALLY!

When someone you are not married to says to you, 'I love you so much I want to go to bed with you' read it as 'I LOVE YOU SO MUCH I WANT TO DESTROY YOU' and run for your life.

Learn self control early in life or else you will never ever learn it. Self-discipline!

A disciplined life orders his life.

It was George Washington who said, 'Discipline is the soul of an army; it makes small numbers formidable, procures success to the weak and confers esteem to all.'

"Self-discipline is the ability to make yourself do what you should do, when you should do it, whether you feel like it or not." - Elbert Hubbard, author and lecturer

Looking at the life of Paul the apostle, a profound leader, we see a clear display of the virtues of self-discipline.

He said in 1 Corinthians 6:12, 'All things are lawful unto me, but all things are not expedient: all things are lawful for me, **but I will not be brought under the power of any.'**

Then in 1 Corinthians 10:23, he said, 'All things are lawful for me, but all things are not expedient: all things are lawful for me, **but all things edify not.'** [**Not all things are beneficial**]

The word expedient is described as appropriate: appropriate, advisable, or useful in a situation that requires action or advantageous: advantageous for practical rather than moral reasons. **So, some things don't have to be morally wrong to be the wrong thing to do.** It's just inappropriate, inadvisable, not useful or advantageous for practical reasons more than moral reasons.

CHARACTERISTICS OF A DISCIPLINED LIFE:

1. A disciplined life places greater value on essentials.

2. It orders its priorities intelligibly.

3. It operates by schedule.

4. It functions without requiring supervision.

5. It makes the most of its time.

6. It takes discipline to be distinguished.

7. If you leave your life to chance, you don't have a chance.

8. "Without discipline there is no life at all." - Katharine Hepburn

9. If you operate by whatever comes your way, you don't get anything accomplished by the end of any day.

10. Discipline runs a schedule that tells him what time he gets up, what he does between the first and second hour, what he does between the second and third hour, the third and fourth hour, fifth and sixth hour, etc.

11. A disciplined person RUNS A SCHEDULE THAT CONNOTES A MAN ON A MISSION. Someone once asked my spiritual father, 'How do you get time to read?' He

answered with a question, 'How do you get time to eat?' He continued, 'How can you schedule your eating time without scheduling your reading time or praying time?'

12. Discipline puts you on a lifestyle of schedules. You know what each day is supposed to deliver and you work at it conscientiously. So no matter where you are today, discipline can transform your destiny. The students who fail in school, failed not because they were poor, they failed because they were disorganized, disorderly, without an orderly program and doing things as it happens.

13. You never find a distinguished man who is not disciplined.

14. It takes an orderly life to enjoy progress. Paul said I will remain committed only to what things are expedient. I will do only those things that are expedient.

That is the law of Discipline.

When as a Christian or at a young age or in courtship, you don't discipline yourself and end up having sex before marriage you end up suspecting each other of infidelity, unfaithfulness and foul play.

WHOEVER CAN COMMIT FORNICATION CAN ALSO COMMIT ADULTERY!

If you don't build certain defence mechanisms into your system and live by certain cardinal principles backed by

God's power, self-discipline, focus and self-control now, you may go to work and find a woman more loving and caring than your wife or a man more loving and affectionate than your husband and fall for them destroying your destiny in the process.

ALWAYS REMEMBER THIS SAYING: **'When wealth is lost, nothing is lost, when health is lost, something is lost, but when character is lost, all is lost.' - Billy Graham**

IF YOU PLAY GAMES BEFORE YOUR MARRIAGE, YOU WILL PLAY GAMES IN AND AFTER MARRIAGE!

Realistically, just because you are married does not mean that your wife is the most beautiful woman you will ever see or your husband the most handsome. IT IS SELF CONTROL AND SELF-DISCIPLINE THAT WILL KEEP YOU AND HELP YOU TO DIFFERENTIATE AND PRIORITISE TO STAY FAITHFUL TO YOUR SPOUSE.

IT IS COMMITMENT THAT MAKES YOU STICK TO ONE PERSON AT A TIME!

LOVE IS A DISCIPLINE! YOU NEED TO DISCIPLINE YOURSELF TO BE AND TO REMAIN IN LOVE WITH ONE PERSON AND ONE PERSON ALONE!

Haven't you heard of men with many wives like King Solomon? So, it can happen.

Discipline, self-control, self-discipline, self-preservation for destiny, dedication, devotion, obedience, focus on destiny, perfect love and the fear of God is what preserves you and keeps you on the narrow way.

Isaiah 52:11-12, 'Depart ye, depart ye, go ye out from thence, touch no unclean thing; go ye out of the midst of her; be ye clean, that bear the vessels of the LORD. For ye shall not go out with haste, nor go by flight: for the LORD will go before you; and the God of Israel will be your rereward.'

When you entertain fretfulness, you will be willing to become someone's third or fourth wife or have a child without a husband just for a council flat or housing association building in the UK. You sell yourself short when you don't discover who you really are. But when you discover your purpose [why you are here] when you discover your potential [gifts, strengths] and discover you are the head and not the tail above only and not beneath [Deuteronomy 28:13] and are pursuing destiny, you discover you are the best and so you settle for nothing less than God's best for you.

HOW DOES GOD BRING YOUR PARTNER?

PRACTICAL STEPS: Genesis 2:18; Songs 1:16-17; 4:9-10; Isaiah 30:20-21; 48:17

1. God does not operate in a vacuum. Any faith that makes God absolutely responsible for the outcome of one's destiny is an irresponsible faith. You must be

involved in the choice of your marriage partner, how you turn out and what you ultimately become in life in conjunction with God.

Psalm 32:8-9, 'I will instruct thee and teach thee in the way which thou shalt go: I will guide thee with mine eye. Be ye not as the horse, or as the mule, which have no understanding: whose mouth must be held in with bit and bridle, lest they come near unto thee.'

2. HE WILL GUIDE YOU WHEN YOU GET HIM INVOLVED!

3. TRUSTING GOD FOR A PARTNER DOES NOT MEAN BEING BLANK, ALOOF OR SHIFTING INTO A VACUUM!

Just as you trust God for everything else and receive it by faith, trusting God for a partner is also by faith. There are no magical or spectacular manifestations like dreams or visions; at least not for majority of people.

4. Whatever your mind is pre-occupied with, you will dream about it.

21 FACTS ABOUT RIGHT/WRONG THINKING / RIGHT/WRONG THOUGHTS:

YOU GRAVITATE TOWARDS WHAT YOU THINK OF AND THINK ON THE MOST!

1. How you think determines who you are.

2. What occupies your mind and what you think of means more than anything else in your life.

3. You gravitate towards the one you think of and think about the most and even dream about them.

4. Your thought-life will determine what you invest in, what you work at or towards, spend more on and more time on, how much you earn, where you live, and what you become in life.

5. Your life today is a result of your thinking yesterday.

6. Your life tomorrow will be determined by what you think today. **John Maxwell said: "….. That which determines the success of a church or any organization's growth more than any other ingredient is what you think you can do. If you think you can, you can. If you think you are, you are."**

7. What enters your mind and occupies your thought process will somewhere, sometime come out of your mouth.

8. **You always head in the direction of your predominant thoughts.**

9. You become what you think about often.

10. Therefore you become what you think about. It has been said, 'Be careful about what you set your heart on for you'll surely get it.'

11. Be careful about what occupies your mind, because it will greatly determine what you'll become tomorrow.

12. Your future is determined by your today.

13. The secret of your future lies in your daily routine.

14. The new birth is the first thing that changes your life.

15. The second step to becoming the person you want to be is changing your thought-life.

16. You can literally change your life by beginning to think different thoughts. **If you desire a mental 'spring cleaning' I suggest you check the following areas:**
   - In what type of environment do you live?

   - Your thoughts reflect what you were given by your environment.

   - What are you doing with your free time?

   - How you spend the time i.e. your own will greatly determine what you think about. No doubt about it: Satan brings his greatest temptations to people when they have time on their hands.

   - It takes discipline of character and proper goals to

handle correctly the extra hours given to an individual in our society.

- What do you do with your spare time? You must understand the importance of filling your free time with tools that will help you think right.

- Who are your closest friends / associations?

- The people you associate with will greatly determine how and what you think.

17. You can change your life by changing your thinking.

18. You can change your thinking by changing your knowledge base or the input of knowledge you take in and its quality.

19. You can change your thinking by changing your environment, the use of your free time and your associations.

20. Use this as the guideline to be applied in your thought-life: Think thoughts that are true, just, honest, pure, lovely, of good report, worthy of praise. Think on these things. (Philippians 4:6-8)

21. Do your best to make it your standard for selecting friends, filling your free time with healthy, productive, value-adding, wealth-generating thoughts and changing your surroundings.

5. REMEMBER: GOD DOES NOT FORCE PEOPLE ON OTHERS BECAUSE WHEN IT COMES TO MARRIAGE, THE WILL OF THE PERSON IS

INVOLVED AND BECOMES VITAL. FOR INSTANCE, GOD PRESENTED EVE TO ADAM, NOT GAVE EVE TO ADAM COMPULSORILY FOR ADAM TO BLAME GOD FOR WHAT WENT WRONG. God did not make the choice for him. **You cannot blame anyone for the choice you make of a husband or a wife.**

6. God will do everything in His will and power to make the right person come your way (Isaiah 48:17) but you eventually make the decision to take that which is presented to you or reject it in favour of another. (Deuteronomy 30:19)

7. Where there is a manifestation, it must be dual – God must have worked from both ends and you must be convinced she is the one and he also, that you are the one.

8. Be mindful of those who come around forcing people on you without your power to choose, your involvement or conviction. Human beings have a choice. When it comes to us, God guides us but leaves us to choose. Whatever you are not confident about is not right. It must bear witness with your spirit that it is right. (Joshua 24:15)

9. Seek counsel from right sources like your Pastor, credible mentors, marriages that are worth emulating because in a multitude of counsel [counselors] there is safety. Proverbs 11:14, 'Where no counsel is, the people fall: but in the multitude of counsellors there is safety.'

10. WARNING LIGHTS!!! When you have countless number

of sound, loving, mature, well-meaning people telling you to be careful, be careful – you may be making the wrong choice which culminates in bad decisions.

11. Don't just marry on the grounds of love only, or pity, compassion, feeling sorry or sympathy. This is your life not a charity show.

12. REMEMBER: Love or falling in love is not the only basis for marriage because you can love or fall in love with the wrong person or more than one person. (1 Kings 11:3)

a. Marriage is about destiny.
b. Marriage is about long term commitment.
c. Marriage is for life until death do you part.
d. Marriage is a covenant agreement and that is why you cannot enter it blindly or break a marriage – what God hath joined/put together let no man put asunder (Matthew 19:6; Mark 10:9)
e. Marriage is full-time commitment and allegiance and that is why you cannot run after any kind of man or woman who shows the slightest or deepest interest in you, compliments you, demonstrates love, kindness, towards you or gives you gifts or excess attention.

You can fall in love with or love the wrong person like a thief, murderer, drug addict or someone's husband or wife. [It's possible]

KNOW THE DIFFERENCE:

13. LOVE VS. LIKE: The fact that you like someone does not mean you love them or are in love with them and vice versa so the difference must be clear. **NOTE: There are people whom you can have a very good relationship with as friends but can never marry. IT WON'T WORK! WHY? YOU ARE NOT MEANT FOR EACH OTHER!**

There is a difference between loving someone and liking someone and when it comes to marriage, both must be in operation because you don't feel love all the time. So, if you don't like them or can't stand them at a time you don't feel love, you are in serious trouble.

14. INFATUATION VS. LOVE: Just because your heart jumps by speaking to or hearing from or at the sight of someone does not mean you should jump into a relationship and commit. When your heart begins to jump at the sight of someone, think. Some could be **infatuation. INFATUATION IS DECEPTIVE AND SHORT TERM; TRUE LOVE IS LASTING/LONG TERM.**

15. LOVE VS. LUST: Love gives; lust takes. Love heals; lust wounds and hurts. Have you heard the saying? **Hurt people, hurt people! HURT PEOPLE END UP HURTING OTHER PEOPLE ALMOST WITHOUT FAIL!**

16. When you are going to get married, ask questions – vital questions, serious questions even if **[especially if]** you are born again. [Order my book: 200 Questions you must ask, investigate and know before you say, 'I DO' from www. houseofjudah.org.uk]

The fact that both of you are Christians [born again] by itself, does not guarantee success and longevity in any relationship more so, marriage.

17. Find out about the person's background.

18. Check their character traits because there are vital things that love or romance will cover your eyes from noticing only for you to marry and discover you married a monster.

REMEMBER: Most of those who break up after a while were actually really in love from the onset but failed to investigate certain facts about their intended spouses clouding it with love and romance. ROMANCE CLOUDS FOCUS!

Some will pretend to you during courtship. You need discernment. Some will never reveal their true identity or show you their true colour until they've gotten you where they wanted you in the first place or gotten what they wanted from you.

So: FRIENDSHIP – THE COURTSHIP PERIOD IS VERY NECESSARY.

19. Don't marry an idiot or do business with a crook - investigate.

20. Don't marry out of pity or sympathy for anyone; it could be highly detrimental to your future.

INVESTIGATIVE JOURNALISM TO MAKING THE RIGHT CHOICE!!

120 MANDATORY QUESTIONS TO ASK AND NOT SHY AWAY FROM, OBLIGATIONS TO MEET, THINGS TO DO, CONSIDER, THINK ABOUT & INVESTIGATE:

1. Don't marry out of pity for a woman who has children with no father. Find out why there is no father in the house, dead or alive.

2. If it's the man, find out what happened to the mother of the child or children.

3. Is he a wife-beater or abuser which led to the woman running off?

4. Is the woman a cantankerous woman?

5. Find out the character of that man or woman who you desire to marry – what are their weaknesses/shortcomings: anger, bad temper, selfish, greedy, procrastinator, argumentative, childishness, throwing tantrums, other serious problems like insanity in the family, diseases like sickle cell anemia, etc.

6. CHRONIC DISEASES IN THE FAMILY; SERIOUS NOTE: SOME PEOPLE GENETICALLY DO NOT BLEND WITH OTHER PEOPLE. SO, EVEN THOUGH YOU LOVE THEM OR ARE IN LOVE WITH THEM, YOU CANNOT MARRY THEM [except by divine instructions and the spirit of faith not blind faith].

YOU CANNOT MARRY THEM [Faith not withstanding]: Such as asthmatics marrying asthmatics; sickle cell anemia marrying another with sickle cell anemia. Despite faith and God's healing power, apply wisdom and seek divine direction before you commit.

7. FAMILY HISTORY

8. MONEY MATTERS [how they handle money]

9. STABILITY OR UNSTABLE FAMILY BACKGROUND

10. Does the person you intend to marry respect their parents or are rude, speaks rudely to the family, cussing or swearing?

11. SOCIAL STANDING: Is the person you are about to marry your size – in your league or way beyond your league [social standing] like the man being a labourer or ordinary gardener or handyman intending to marry a doctor, lawyer, parliamentarian, architect, politician 'by faith' – it may be possible but you must count the cost involved and develop

yourself by sacrificing to make the needed adjustments – don't just look at love.

- You will have to deal with your partner's – his/her insecurities, if any.

12. Think about purpose, dreams, vision.

13. Think about compatibility.

14. Do we get on?

15. Do we have same or similar interests or are far apart?

16. Do we like each other? [Friendship - phileo]

17. Do we love each other? [Romance - Eros]

18. Do we have in mind to have a family? [Storge]

19. Is God's love at the centre of this relationship? [Agape -unconditional love]

20. Do they get on with their family or are always at loggerheads or fighting?

21. Does he/she love God or the things of God? [Some pretend just to marry you and later react, rebel and frustrate their partners.]

22. Which direction is your spouse heading – is it the same direction as yours?

23. What are your plans for the future – what are theirs?

24. Does he/she like what you like?

25. Are they willing to compromise?

26. What kind of food do they like – can you cook it? What about you?

27. What kind of home do they come from i.e. broken or stable home, happy or sad, troublesome or peaceful?

28. Is he/she an introvert or extrovert and what about you?

29. Does he/she like conversations or staying quiet?

30. What are their interests, do they love extracurricular activities or staying home?

31. Do they love your company or being by themselves?

32. Will they still continue to love or like your company after marriage? How sure are you?

33. What kind of entertainment do you both enjoy or separately?

34. What kind of games, sports, concerts, films, theatre?

35. Do you enjoy outdoor or indoor sports/activities?

36. What kind of food, clothing, hair style, shoes, home decor do both of you like or dislike?

37. Are both of you close to your family or distant? i.e Do both of you come from a closely-knit family or divided (dysfunctional) family?

38. Were you [both of you] raised by a two-parent family or single-parent family?

39. Are you marrying them out of conviction or convenience?

40. Are you marrying them because of what to get from them or what to give to them?

41. Are you going to give this relationship 50/50 or 100/100? Do you know the difference?

42. Are you marrying them to get your immigration status or citizenship?

43. Is this relationship to your advantage, their advantage or both your advantage?

44. Are you signing a prenuptial agreement before you marry? Why?

45. Who stands to gain more or lose more in this relationship when you marry?

46. Are both of you spendthrift or good with handling money?

47. Are both of you extravagant or moderate – do you wear only designer clothing or others?

48. Are both of you ready for joint accounts or separate accounts?

49. Do you or your partner always want to buy or save/invest?

50. Are both of you selfless or selfish?

51. Are both of you prone to being jealous or secure?

52. What do you hate most or like most in each other and in life generally? Does your prospective partner know?

53. Do you know what gets on his/her 'last' nerves?

54. Do you know when to be quiet and when to speak with your prospective partner?

55. Do you know what grieves them or excites them the most?

56. Are you walking on eggshells around them or free?

57. Are you allowed to express your opinions freely around

each other?

58. Do you get on with their parents, relatives and family or pretend?

59. Are both of you envious or satisfied with who you are?

60. Do you compare yourself with others or your purpose/ destiny?

61. Are both of you secure or insecure?

62. Are both of you easily satisfied or hardly satisfied?

63. Can you stand being alone [by yourself] when your prospective partner has to be away for a while?

64. Are you over-protective of what is yours or liberal?

65. Are you generous or stingy?

66. Do they observe the wind to sow or just give? (Ecclesiastes 11)

67. Can both of you still give, support or meet your financial obligations to your parents/relatives if need be without it creating friction or issues? Have you discussed this?

68. Do you have 'Plan B' if this relationship does not work or are you a stickler?

69. Do both of you or does any of you have an alternative when there is an argument, a disagreement or things don't go your way?

70. Are both of you generally possessive?

71. Are you after each other's money or family inheritance?

72. Are they prone to accidents?

73. Do you have any differences with the person you intend to marry?

74. Are you real with each other or pretentious?

75. Are you argumentative?

76. Are you real or fake?

77. Are you involved in constructive or destructive criticism?

78. Are you a talkative?

79. When it comes to arguments or disagreements, do you always want to win or compromise?

80. Are you keeping things that offend you about your partner till you get married or you voice it out?

81. Do you keep a record of each others' wrongs?

82. Do you have frozen rage?

83. Do you have a habit of bringing up what's in the past when a fresh disagreement comes up?

84. Find out his/her attitude towards children. Do they like children?

85. Do you know if she wants children or is a career woman/man?

86. Will he allow you to pursue your goals and course/degree when you marry?

87. Are the children coming first or education first? Have you discussed this?

88. How many children do you intend to have?

89. Are you going to be independent, unilateral on your decision-making or in consultation with your partner?

90. Are you still thinking like a single person or married?

91. In certain communities or cultures, it is accepted that since the man is the head of the home, he should be older in age, better established in life, taking the leading role and must be secure and that their gift is that of strength and ability to

work and the woman stays at home. Have you considered this notion or discussed this?

92. Are you going to be living in the same country or one will be living afar off because of work?

93. Are you going to leave and stay out of your matrimonial home when you have an argument or stay put?

94. What kind of man is he? Does he get tired easily? Is he decisive?

a. An easily tired man will not be a good husband.

b. An indecisive man is controlled remotely by someone [parents, friends, past ties].

c. A man must be decisive, tough, visionary, kindhearted, loving, responsible, fair and firm.

d. A man must have sight, foresight insight, hindsight and far-sight. WOMEN BECOME MEN WHEN MEN STOP BEING MEN. [***For additional insight on what marriage is, order our newest books: 101 TIPS FOR A GREAT MARRIAGE and WHAT HUSBANDS WANT AND WHAT WIVES 'REALLY' WANT from our website: www.houseofjudah.org.uk]

95. What kind of woman is she?

96. Is he/she a talkative, thief, proud, arrogant, rude, etc?

97. Is she demanding and never satisfied or content? A demanding wife will turn you into a thief and a robber. She will pressurize you to connive, condone, bribe, to steal to meet that need. She will force you to seek for political asylum when you are not a politician or refugee.

98. Is she cantankerous? A contentious wife is as brokenness of tooth. - Proverbs 25:19

A cantankerous woman will make you want to pull your hair and your teeth out and that's what you will feel like doing to her because of the aggravation from her unreasonable demands and expectations.

99. Does she duplicate what she sees in other people's houses in yours?

100. Is she a quarrelsome woman?

101. Is she covetous?

102. Is she greedy?

103. How do they conduct themselves at home? They will do the same in yours.

104. Are there murderers or paedophiles [pedophiles] in their family?

105. How many marriage break ups are there?

106. Are they from a broken, disintegrated home or integrated home?

107. Are they tidy or untidy at home?

108. Do they dress up neatly or shabby or anyhow?

109. Are they clean?

110. Do they have right motives or evil intentions toward you?

111. Does he/she compete with you or complete you?

112. Is he/she a tither or not? [Giving ten percent of their income to God and their church – if not don't marry them – period. Why? A person who can steal from God can steal from you. (Malachi 3:6-12)]

113. Do you compete with each other or complete each other?

114. Are you honest with each other or pretentious for fear of losing each other?

115. Are you truthful with each other?

116. What are your weaknesses and strengths i.e. both of you?

117. What character flaws do you both have?

118. Are you going to be committed for life?

119. What do both of you intend to be known for?

120. What legacy do you intend to leave behind you?

[For additional insight on singles, marriage and relationships, order our newest books: 101 TIPS FOR A GREAT MARRIAGE, WHAT HUSBANDS WANT AND WHAT WIVES 'REALLY' WANT, 50 Common Mistakes Singles Make and 200 QUESTIONS YOU MUST ASK, INVESTIGATE AND KNOW BEFORE YOU SAY 'I DO' from our bookshop or our website: **www.houseofjudah.org.uk**]

FROM THE ABOVE, YOU DISCOVER WHY LOVE IS NOT THE ONLY BASIS FOR MARRIAGE.

'The hearts of men are too deep to uncover, the minds of men are too unstable to depend on and the words of men are too sweet to doubt.' - BISHOP OYEDEPO

ADVICE TO PROSPECTIVE COUPLES & THOSE IN COURTSHIP

1. Add other virtues to love like going for knowledge, understanding, insight and wisdom. (2 Peter 1:3-11)

2. LOVE MUST NOT BE BLIND TO REALITIES!

3. Scripture says dwell with your wives according to knowledge not blind with love.

4. CONTRARY TO WHAT PEOPLE SAY, THAT: 'LOVE IS BLIND', LOVE IS NOT BLIND; LOVE MUST SEE CLEARLY BEFORE IT LEAPS!

Read to know more about people and the subject of marriage

before jumping into it. [For additional insight on what marriage is, order our five newest books on relationships: 101 TIPS FOR A GREAT MARRIAGE and WHAT HUSBANDS WANT AND WHAT WIVES 'REALLY' WANT, 50 COMMON MISTAKES SINGLES MAKE and 200 QUESTIONS YOU MUST ASK, INVESTIGATE AND KNOW BEFORE YOU SAY 'I DO' from our website: www.houseofjudah.org.uk]

5. Don't expend all your energies, emotions, time and resources to do all the dating before marriage; reserve most dating till after marriage.

6. Go to your intended partner's home and investigate all this before you marry them.

7. Your commitments to your families just in case your parents are not working should be thoroughly discussed lest after you marry, you are barred or your partner puts an injunction on your remitting your family.

8. In certain cultures, some are the bread-winners in the family and come from backgrounds and still have family attachments and obligations they must continue to meet even after marriage so this must be understood and thoroughly discussed so it does not bring friction.

9. You don't marry and start giving your husband instructions; so, count the cost.

10. Don't argue and if you do, try not to say anything to offend your partner or you will regret saying later.

11. Avoid manipulation [controlling your partner emotionally, sexually or physically].

12. Go for adequate counseling, keep reading books and watching DVDs and listen to messages on relationships – how they work.

13. When you meet someone today, advisedly, there must be some time lapse for counseling, these investigations, courtship and getting to know each other building friendships before getting married – ADVISEDLY.

14. Sit yourselves down and talk to each other – COMMUNICATE.

15. Talk about SEX AND MONEY – Get my books.

16. Tell each other what you are here for, having first discovered it before meeting them or take time to discover and tell each other what you desire to achieve in life, where you want to go, settle, travel to and end up in life.

17. Talk about your dreams – both dreams and how they can work together in harmony to complete both of you and empower you to fulfill destiny.

18. Talk about the costs involved and the sacrifices to be made.

19. Head towards one goal and assist, help, encourage and

empower each other to achieve and attain those goals.

20. Commit yourselves to the institution of marriage and each other.

21. Have the future in mind during courtship [when you are moving with someone].

22. INVESTIGATE AND FAMILIARIZE YOURSELF WITH THE NECESSARY REQUIREMENTS, DEMANDS, DOWRIES FROM YOUR PARTNERS' FAMILY ABOUT YOUR OBLIGATIONS BEFORE ASKING FOR THEIR HAND IN MARRIAGE, ENGAGING AND MARRYING THEM AND MEET THOSE OBLIGATIONS. NO RINGY, NO DINGY!!!

23. BETTER TO BREAK A RELATIONSHIP BEFORE MARRIAGE THAN TO WAIT UNTIL YOU GET INTO MARRIAGE AND THINK OF DIVORCE. [Refer to chapter nine on what you should know about divorce before getting married]

24. You can break up even after an engagement if you realize or discover you've made a mistake, the wrong choice or decision.

25. BETTER SAFE THAN NEVER!

26. PREVENTION IS BETTER THAN CURE!

27. IT IS NEVER LATE TO BE RIGHT BECAUSE MARRIAGE IS THE NEXT THING TO HEAVEN ON EARTH OR LIFE IMPRISONMENT WITH HARD LABOUR!

28. You save yourself a whole lot of heartache by getting it right the first time.

29. Don't get involved with anyone who will abort your vision, purpose and destiny.

30. The main purpose of God for your life is not getting married first. IT IS TO FULFIL DESTINY! YOUR MARRIAGE PARTNER IS TO HELP YOU FULFIL THAT DESTINY, NOT THE OTHER WAY ROUND! The whole duty of man is to fear God and obey His commands and fulfill his vision. (Ecclesiastes 12:13; 1 John 3:8; Jeremiah 29:11; Proverbs 29:18; 22:29; 27:8)

31. What a person is committed to, if you are not committed to the same thing, you will not understand them, cannot marry them or you will be frustrated. How can two walk together except they be agreed? (Amos 3:3)

32. Your greatest enemy is the one who takes your eyes off God and your destiny/purpose/vision.

33. GO AFTER THE ONE YOU LOVE ON CONDITION HE/SHE IS GOD'S CHOICE FOR YOU.

Songs 3:1-5, 'By night on my bed I sought him whom my soul loveth: I sought him, but I found him not. I will rise now, and go about the city in the streets, and in the broad ways I will seek him whom my soul loveth: I sought him, but I found him not. The watchmen that go about the city found me: to whom I said, Saw ye him whom my soul loveth? It was but a little that I passed from them, but I found him whom my soul loveth: I held him, and would not let him go, until I had brought him into my mother's house, and into the chamber of her that conceived me. I charge you, O ye daughters of Jerusalem, by the roes, and by the hinds of the field, that ye stir not up, nor awake my love, till he please.'

34. AFTER MEETING THE REQUIREMENTS: GET MARRIED THE RIGHT WAY – verse 6 to the end.

'Who is this that cometh out of the wilderness like pillars of smoke, perfumed with myrrh and frankincense, with all powders of the merchant? Behold his bed, which is Solomon's; threescore valiant men are about it, of the valiant of Israel. They all hold swords, being expert in war: every man hath his sword upon his thigh because of fear in the night. King Solomon made himself a chariot of the wood of Lebanon. He made the pillars thereof of silver, the bottom thereof of gold, the covering of it of purple, the midst thereof being paved with love, for the daughters of Jerusalem. Go forth, O ye daughters of Zion, and behold king Solomon with the crown wherewith his mother crowned him in the day of his espousals, and in the day of the gladness of his heart.'

35. STAY MARRIED!

36. HOW TO PRAISE YOUR WIFE!
Songs 4 & 6:4-10

37. Troubled evenings or missing your partner.
Songs 3&5; 7:1-9, 10-13

38. What to say of your husband.
Songs 5:9-6:3; 7:10-13; 8:6-7

39. Boast about knowing where he is.
Songs 6:1-3

40. How to invite him to bed before the night.
Songs 4:16; 7:10-13

PRAYER:
OUR PRAYER IS THAT GOD WILL HELP YOU MAKE THE RIGHT CHOICES LEADING TO GOOD DECISIONS AND KEEP YOU FROM MAKING WRONG CHOICES THAT LEAD TO BAD DECISIONS. AMEN! (Psalm 1:1-3; 37:4-6)

OUR PRAYER IS THAT YOU WILL NOT FOLLOW YOUR EMOTIONS TO LEAD YOU ASTRAY BUT YOU WILL FOLLOW PURPOSE, DESTINY, VISION, DIVINE DIRECTION, GOD'S WILL FOR YOUR LIFE. (Isaiah 48:17)

OUR PRAYER IS THAT GOD WILL LEAD YOU TO MEET THE RIGHT APPOINTED PERSON AT THE RIGHT TIME AT THE RIGHT PLACE FOR YOUR APPOINTED DESTINY (Isaiah 30:20-21; Genesis 3:16; 1 Corinthians 7:14,34; 14:35; 2 Corinthians 11:2; Ephesians 5:23,25))

OUR PRAYER IS YOU WILL FOLLOW GODLY COUNSEL AND WISDOM AND FULFIL GOD'S PURPOSE FOR YOUR LIFE AFTER OR AS YOU FIND A GOOD WIFE. (Proverbs 5:18; 18:22; 19:14; Ecclesiastes 9:9; Ephesians 5:28; Colossians 3:19: 1 Peter 3:1-7)

No Ringy, No Dingy

Chapter
Twelve

THE CHECKLIST

100 KEY CHARACTERISTICS TO LOOK FOR IN A POTENTIAL SPOUSE

THERE IS NO NEW THING UNDER THE SUN; LEARN FROM THOSE WHO MADE RIGHT CHOICES:

Ecclesiastes 1:7-11,

'All the rivers run into the sea; yet the sea is not full; unto the place from whence the rivers come, thither they return again. All things are full of labour; man cannot utter it: the eye is not satisfied with seeing, nor the ear filled with hearing. The thing that hath been, it is that which shall be; and that which is done is that which shall be done: and there is no new thing under the sun. Is there any thing whereof it may be said, See, this is new? it hath been already of old time, which was before us.'

YOU ARE NOT THE FIRST PERSON TO GET MARRIED; OTHERS HAVE GONE AHEAD OF YOU: LISTEN TO GOOD COUNSEL:

Proverbs 11:14, 'Where no counsel is, the people fall: but in the multitude of counsellors there is safety.'

WHAT TO AIM FOR IN THE CHOICE OF A MARRIAGE PARTNER:

1. Destiny-fulfilment [One you can fulfil destiny/purpose with].
2. Visionary.
3. Purpose-driven.
4. Knows where he/she is going and how to get there.
5. God-fearing.
6. Loves God and the Word intensely.
7. Reliable.
8. No negative or destructive habits or addictions [Non-smoker]
9. Good Manners.
10. Smart investor in kingdom and productive ventures.
11. Respectful.
12. Loving and Affectionate.
13. Sincere and honest.
14. One you both love and like.
15. Energetic.
16. Strong and confident.
17. Emotionally secure.

18. Good-looking or Pretty [beautiful both within and without].
19. One who understands and exhibits Unconditional love [Agape], Phileo [Friendship love], Storge [Family Love] and Eros [Romantic and Sexual love].
20. Good communicator.
21. Funny [Great sense of humour].
22. Walks and lives by faith.
23. Financially stable or a planner [Financial stability].
24. Smart/astute, smartly dressed and in outlook with good taste/clean.
25. Strong and stable emotionally and physically.
26. Matured.
27. Not lazy but hard working.
28. Good conflict management skills.
29. Good people skills.
30. Ambitious [based on vision within original purpose].
31. Faithful and loyal.
32. Dependable.
33. Punctual.
34. Responsible.
35. Engages his mental faculties well to create wealth and make sound productive decisions.
36. Things in common.
37. Passionate to me and about his/her assignment in life.
38. Addicted to personal/self-development.
39. A Believer [same faith belief system – one direction] (Amos 3:3).
40. Goals and family-oriented.
41. Whose love is as strong as death. (Songs 8:6)

42. Physically attractive and compatible.
43. The capacity for true intimacy.
44. Committed.
45. Trusting.
46. A person of impeccable character.
47. Helpful.
48. My best Friend.
49. Kind.
50. Patient and understanding.
51. Acceptance.
52. Cordiality and agreement over money. (Amos 3:3)
53. Not difficult to live with or stubborn/obstinate/rude.
54. Humble and meek.
55. Fidelity [Abstinence from Infidelity].
56. Agreements over children's training and development.
57. Not prone to physical or mental abuse.
58. Not distractive or a distracter.
59. Unconditional love, stability and consistency.
60. Generous [Great provider and giver].
61. Confident and courageous.
62. Warm.
63. Blessed and highly favoured.
64. A reader and productive thinker.
65. Willing to grow and develop daily.
66. Caring.
67. Supportive.
68. Works on their annoying habits.
69. Not grumpy and stingy.
70. Has the potential for loving, having and
    being responsible for, to and with our children.

71. Exhibits and demonstrates the **essential ingredients of Love** (The Five Love Languages: Words of Affirmation; Quality Time; Gifts; Acts of Service; Physical Touch).

72. Fulfils his/her obligation emotionally and sexually to me.

73. One who loves people.

74. Takes initiatives.

75. Creates a home to be proud of and a sense of security.

76. A person who will help me to make the marriage work and give his or her all for the betterment of the marriage.

77. A person who is stable and kind.

78. A person who is slow to anger, wrath and to speaking guile.

79. A person who is a good worker and who has a good job or is seriously looking for one within his/her purpose.

80. Someone who understands the art of compromise.

81. Someone who values honesty, respect and loyalty in self and others.

82. Someone who ISN'T high maintenance, and is committed.

83. Someone who does not faint under pressure.

84. Someone who can still love my friends and family because they're a part of me.

85. Someone who isn't afraid to be authoritative when he needs to be.

86. Someone who is gentle to old people and babies.

87. Someone who's prepared to be locked in with a single person for life.

88. Someone willing to give up a great deal of freedom to be with me.
89. Someone willing to consult on most issues if not all.
90. Someone willing to have to work to maintain and build their human qualities and character.
91. A person who will be a good mother or father.
92. Someone who's always there for us both.
93. Someone who will help us get more for our efforts.
94. Someone who is decisive.
95. Someone devoted to me alone.
96. Someone with a generational mindset and global world view.
97. Different from me but whose company I greatly enjoy.
98. Offers Assurance and security.
99. One who offers long-term companionship and commitment for life.
100. Loves God's house and is active, committed, loyal and faithful there.

THE GREATEST GIFT

If you want to take advantage of the contents of this message by asking God to give you power to lead, from which Adam fell, you need to give your life to Jesus Christ. If you have never met or experienced a definite encounter with Jesus Christ, you can know Him today. You can make your life right with Him by accepting Him as your personal Lord and Saviour by praying the following prayer out loud where you are. Pray this prayer with me now:

PRAYER FOR SALVATION: 'O God, I ask you to forgive me for my sins. I believe You sent Jesus to die on the cross for me and confess it with my mouth. I receive Jesus Christ as my personal Lord and Saviour and confess Him as Lord of my life and I give my life willingly to Him now. Thank you Lord for saving me and for making me a new person in Jesus' Name, (2 Corinthians 5:17) Amen.'

If you prayed this prayer, you have now become a child of God (John 1:12) and I welcome you to the family of God. Please let me know about your decision for Jesus by writing to me. I would like to send you some free literature to help you in your new walk with the Lord. So please write to me at the following address:

Correspondence address:
Michael Hutton-Wood,
House of Judah (Praise) Ministries
P. O. Box 1226,
Croydon. CR9 6DG. UK.

Or call:
Within the UK:
0208 689 6010, 07956 815 714
Outside the UK:
+44 208 689 6010, +44 7956 815 714

Alternatively Email us at:
Email: info@houseofjudah.org.uk
michaelhutton-wood@fsmail.net
Or visit us at: Website: www.houseofjudah.org.uk

Watch our 24hour internet TV experience on
www.judahtv.org

OTHER BOOKS AND LEADERSHIP MANUALS BY AUTHOR

1. A Must For Every New Convert
2. You Need To Do The Ridiculous In Order To Experience The Miraculous
3. 175 Reasons Why You Cannot And Will Not Fail In Life
4. What To Do In The Darkest Hour Of Your Trial [125 Bible Truths You Must Know, BELIEVE, REMEMBER, CONFESS AND DO]
5. Why You should Pray And How You should Pray For Your Pastor and Your Church Daily
6. 200 Questions You Must Ask, Investigate And Know Before You Say 'I Do'
7. I Shall Rise Again
8. How to negotiate your desired future with today's currency
9. Leadership Secrets
10. Leadership Nuggets
11. Leadership Capsules
12. What is Ministry
13. Generating Finances For Ministry
14. 101 Tips For a Great Marriage
15. What Husbands Want And What Wives 'REALLY' Want
16. My Daily Bible Reading Guide.

TRAINING MANUALS FOR IMPACTFUL LEADERSHIP & EFFECTIVE MINISTRY

Academy 101 [House Of Judah Academy Curriculum]
Ministry 101
Leadership 101
Kingdom Prosperity 101 From School Of Kingdom Prosperity & Financial Management
Pastoral Leadership 101 From School Of Impactful Pastoral Leadership
Prescriptions For Fulfilling Your Ministry
To order copies of any of these books, ministry or leadership manuals or for a product catalog of other literature, audiotapes and CDs, DVDs, write to: Michael Hutton-Wood Ministries, P. O. Box 1226, Croydon. CR9 6DG. UK. or [in the UK call]
- 0208 689 6010; [outside UK call] + 442086896010
You can also place your order online as you visit our website: www.houseofjudah.org.uk
You can also email us at:
Email: info@houseofjudah.org.uk;
or michaelhutton-wood@fsmail.net

GLOBAL INITIATIVES AND MINISTRIES WITHIN THE MINISTRY

TV MINISTRY IN THE UK
Watch Leadership Secrets on KICC TV
SKY Channel 594
Tuesday & Thursday – 3pm & Saturday 5.30pm
Monday-Friday 2pm on FAITH TV
Sky channel 593 & Saturday 3.30pm

LOG ON AND WATCH OUR INTERNET TV
PROGRAM on WWW.JUDAHTV.ORG
Anytime - anywhere.
Featuring the:
Teaching Channel
Motivation Channel
Leadership Channel
Family/ Relationships Channel
Upcoming Events/ Products
WATCH US ON YouTube and AUDIO STREAMING
EVERY WEEK
@ www.houseofjudah.org.uk

PARTNERING WITH A GLOBAL MINISTRY WITHIN A MINISTRY

Michael Hutton-Wood Ministries (The HUTTON-WOOD WORLD OUTREACH MINISTRY) is the apostolic, missions, world outreach, and evangelistic wing of the House of Judah (Praise) Ministries with a mission to God's end time church and the nations of the earth. This ministry was born out of a strong God-given mandate to reach, touch and impact the nations of the earth with the gospel of Christ and bring back divine order, discipline, integrity, godly character, excellence and stability to God's people and God's house. It has a strong apostolic mandate to set in order the things that are out of order and lacking in the church [The Body of Christ] – (Titus 1:5).

Its mission is to save the lost at any cost, depopulate hell and populate heaven with souls that have experienced in full, the new birth, renewal of mind, to produce believers walking in the fullness of their Godly inheritance, divine health, prosperity and authority to take their homes, communities, cities and nations for Christ and occupy till Christ returns. It is to raise a people without spot, wrinkle or blemish. The man of God's passion and drive is that as truly as he lives, this earth shall be filled with the knowledge of the glory of the Lord as the waters cover the sea. His determination is not to rest, hold back or keep silent until he sees the body of Christ established as a praise in the earth. (Numbers 14:21; Habakkuk 2:14; Isaiah 62:6-7)

If you would like to join the faithful brethren and partners of this great ministry by becoming a partner as we believe God for ten thousand partners to partner with this vision prayerfully and financially, ask for a copy of the partners' club commitment card by writing to:

Michael Hutton-Wood Ministries
[Hutton-Wood World Outreach]
P. O. Box 1226, Croydon. Surrey.
CR9 6DG. UK.

Alternatively, you can send a monthly contribution by cheque payable to our ministry or donate online at www.houseofjudah.org.uk or request a direct debit mandate or standing order form from your bankers or us made payable to Michael Hutton-Wood Ministries. Call +44 [0] 208 689 6010 for more details. Philippians 4:19 be your portion and experience as you partner with this work and global mandate. Shalom!

GENERATIONAL LEADERSHIP TRAINING INSTITUTE
(The Leaders' Factory)

The Mandate: Raising Generational Leaders, Impacting Nations. The Generational Leadership Training Institute (GLTI) is the Leadership training and mentoring wing of our ministry with a global mandate to raise leaders with a generational thinking mindset, not a now mentality and to fulfil the Law of Explosive Growth – To add growth, lead followers – To multiply, lead leaders.

This is a Bible College, Leadership Training Institute fulfilling the Matthew 9:37-38 mandate of developing and releasing labourers for the end time harvest. We offer fulltime and part time certificate, diploma, degree and short twelve-week courses in biblical studies, counselling, leadership, practical ministry and schools of prosperity. Its aim is to raise leaders who know and live not just by the anointing but by ministerial ethics, leaders who build with a long term mentality, who live today with tomorrow in mind. The mission of this unique educational and impartation institution is to transform followers into generational leaders and its motto is to raise leaders of discipline, integrity, godly character and excellence - D.I.C.E.

For correspondence, full time, part time, online courses, prospectus, fees and registration forms for the next course, call 0208 689 6010 or write to the Registrar, GLTI, P. O. Box 1226, Croydon. CR9 6DG. UK or from outside UK call +44 208 689 6010.

Additional information can be obtained from visiting our website www.houseofjudah.org.uk looking for THE LEADERS FACTORY.

Log on to www.judahtv.org for Leadership Secrets and other teaching.

This is a hutton-wood publication

LEADERS FACTORY INTERNATIONAL

MANDATE: 'In the business of training, developing and raising and releasing more leaders and leaders of leaders.'

'Leaders must be close enough to relate to others, but far enough ahead to motivate them.' – John Maxwell

'You must live with people to know their problems, and live with God in order to solve them.' – P. T. Forsyth

If you, your organisation, college, university, business or church would like to invite Dr. Michael Hutton-Wood for a Motivational-speaking, mentoring or leadership coaching engagement or to organize or hold a Leaders Factory seminar or conference, Leadership Development or Human Capital building seminar, Emerging leaders seminar, Management seminar, Business seminar, Effective people-management, Wealth-creation seminar or training for your workers, leaders, staff, ministers, employers, employees, congregation, youth, etc. you can contact us on 0208 689 6010 [UK]
+44208 689 6010 [OUTSIDE UK].

Alternatively by email at:
- info@houseofjudah.org.uk
- michaelhutton-wood@fsmail.net
or leadersfactoryinternational@yahoo.com
VISIT our website: www.houseofjudah.org.uk
You can watch our internet TV experience www.judahtv. org [Maximizing Destiny and Leadership Secrets].
This is a Hutton-Wood publication

MANDATE:
Releasing Potential - Maximizing Destiny
Raising Generational Leaders - Impacting Nations

SIMPA

SCEPTRE INTERNATIONAL MINISTERS & PASTORS ASSOCIATION

This covenant mandate comes from Genesis 49:10: 'The sceptre [of Leadership] shall not depart from JUDAH, nor a lawgiver from between his feet, until Shiloh come and unto Him shall the gathering of the people be'

Other covenant scriptures backing this mandate are: Isaiah 55:4 & Titus 1:5. We have a leadership assignment to RAISE GENERATIONAL LEADERS TO IMPACT NATIONS BY DISCOVERING MEN/WOMEN AND EMPOWERING THEM TO RELEASE THEIR POTENTIAL TO MAXIMIZE THEIR DESTINY.

SIMPA is a multi-cultural fellowship/network of diverse Christian leaders, pastors and ministers that recognize the need for fathering, covering and mentoring. The heartbeat of the man of God is to pour into the willing and obedient what has made him and keeps making him from what he's learnt from his father in the Lord, his teachers and mentors which is working for him and producing maximally. He said: 'I discovered this secret early: Not to learn from or follow those who make promises but from those who have obtained the promises, proofs and results. REMEMBER: YOU DON'T NEED TO MAKE NOISE TO MAKE NEWS. SO: FOLLOW NEWS-MAKERS NOT NOISE-

MAKERS!'

These are a few of the mindsets of the man of God:

When the students are ready, the teacher will teach.

'YOU NEED FATHERS TO FATHER YOU TO GROW FEATHERS TO FLY.' – Bishop Oyedepo

'Without a father to father you, you can never grow feathers to fly and go further in life, than they went and accomplish more than they did.' – Michael Hutton-Wood

Don't raise money; raise men and you'll have all the money you need to accomplish your assignment.

There is no new thing under the sun – King Solomon

What you desire to attain, become and accomplish in life, someone has accomplished it – find them, follow them, learn from them, sow into them and their resource materials and you will do more than they did and get there faster.

Teachers, Trainers, Mentors and Fathers give you speed/acceleration in every field of endeavour.

Isaac Newton is known to have said the following:

'If I have seen further it has been by standing on the shoulders of those who have gone ahead of me.'

Variant translations: 'Plato is my friend, Aristotle is my friend, but my best friend is truth.'

'Plato is my friend — Aristotle is my friend — truth is a greater friend.'

'If I have seen further it is only by standing on the shoulders of giants.'

Without a reference you can never become a reference.

If you don't refer to anyone no one will refer to you.

Who laid / lays hands on you and what did / do they leave behind?

This is not a money-making venture but rather about covering and empowerment for fulfilment of destiny and assignment within time allocated.

The goal of SIMPA is to spiritually cover, strengthen, equip, empower, train, mentor and encourage and lift up the arms/ hands of both emerging and active [full and part time] pastors, ministers and leaders and by so doing release them to fulfil their respective assignments both in ministry and the market place.

IF YOU WOULD LIKE TO BE A PART OF SIMPA, ASK FOR A REGISTRATION FORM & PAMPHLET FROM OUR INFORMATION DESK in House of Judah or email info@houseofjudah.org.uk or call [in the UK] 0208 689 6010 [outside UK call] + 44 208 689 6010 requesting for SIMPA registration form and pamphlet.

– SEE YOU ON TOP!

Shalom! – Bishop

PARTNERSHIP:
In the UK write or send cheque donations to:
Michael Hutton-Wood Ministries
P. O. Box 1226
Croydon. CR9 6DG. UK.

In the UK Call: 0208 689 6010; 07956 815 714
Outside the UK call: +44 208 689 6010;
+ 44 7956 815 714
Fax: +44 20 8689 3301

Email:
info@houseofjudah.org.uk
michaelhutton-wood@fsmail.net
leadersfactoryinternational@yahoo.com
judah@houseofjudah.freeserve.co.uk

Or visit or donate online at our secure
WEBSITE: www.houseofjudah.org.uk

Watch our 24 hour internet TV experience by logging on
anywhere - anytime @ www.judahtv.org

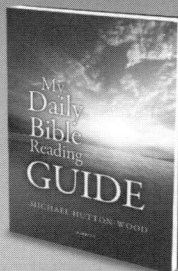

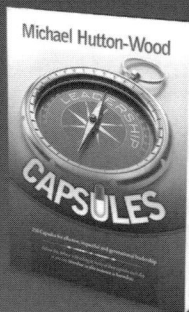

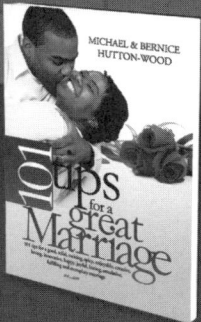

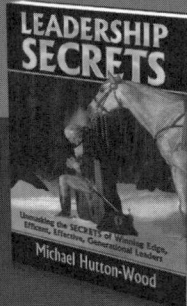

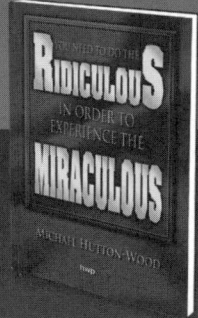

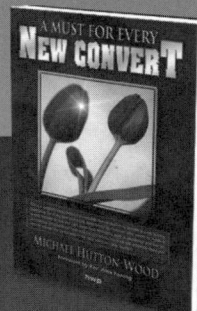